ASSASSINATION

Robert F. Kennedy-1925-1968

ASSASSINATION

Robert F. Kennedy-1925-1968

by the editors of
United Press International and Cowles

edited by Francine Klagsbrun and David C. Whitney

COWLES

STAFF / COWLES EDUCATION CORPORATION

President and Editor David C. Whitney;
Executive Editor Francine Klagsbrun;
Art Director Ronald Gilbert;
Editors: Nat Brandt, Catherine Fauver, Nancy Holmes,
Elizabeth Lieberman; Production Manager Robert F. Hirsch.

STAFF / UNITED PRESS INTERNATIONAL

Vice-President and Executive Editor Francis T. Leary;
Director of Special Projects Harold Blumenfeld; Correspondents:
Milton Benjamin, Myram Borders, Louis Cassels, Ronald G. Cohen,
Mike Feinsilber, Timothy Ferris, Jack Fox, Paul R. Jeschke,
Richard Lerner, John McDonough, George Marder,
Edward O'Connor, Daniel Rapoport, Ed Rogers, Arnold B. Sawislak,
Vernon Scott, De Van L. Shumway, Eliav Simon, Merriman Smith,
Frank Swoboda, Helen Thomas, Ann Wood, Tracy Wood.

Preface

This book is based on the news and picture coverage of Senator Robert F. Kennedy's death and funeral by United Press International.

When Senator Kennedy was felled by a burst of gunfire in Los Angeles at 12:15 A.M. PDT Wednesday, June 5, 1968, UPI staff men were at the scene and moved swiftly to document the story in words, pictures, and audio reports.

UPI photographer Ron Bennett was walking a few steps behind the Senator in the Ambassador Hotel when he heard sounds "like firecrackers or balloons." As a man next to him fell to the floor with blood streaming from his head, Bennett dropped to a crouch. In seconds, the room turned into bedlam. Bennett rapidly took photos of the fallen Kennedy and then turned his camera on accused assassin Sirhan Bishara Sirhan as Kennedy aides wrestled a .22 caliber pistol from Sirhan's hand.

When the shots rang out Joseph St. Amant, veteran Los Angeles staffer, was talking on a telephone near the stage in the Embassy room, dictating Kennedy's victory speech to a special election bureau several blocks away. Shouldering his way through the crowd, St. Amant heard cries of "Bobby's been shot."

It took just moments to confirm the shooting and to race back to the telephone to report the tragedy to the desk headed by Pacific Division News Editor Joe W. Morgan. As Morgan rolled the initial bulletins and urgent adds, a rapid redeployment of the staff was started with reinforcements summoned from San Francisco and Las Vegas.

Ultimately, more than 70 UPI news staffers, photographers, newsfilm and audio reporters were involved in the Los Angeles facets of the story. As the fast-moving story developed, many criss-crossed sprawling downtown Los Angeles to reach Good Samaritan Hospital, where Kennedy died 25½ hours after the shooting, the police station, jail, offices of the Mayor, district attorney, public defender and coroner, and political headquarters of various candidates.

As the hours wore on UPI dispatches of the death of Kennedy, in a tragic reminder of the assassination of his brother, President John F.

7

Kennedy, were transmitted under the bylines of Jack Fox, veteran roving reporter who recently transferred to Los Angeles; Ray Lahr, Washington bureau political analyst; Joseph St. Amant, Los Angeles; Vernon Scott, Hollywood reporter; Paul Jeschke, San Francisco; Myram Borders, Las Vegas; De Van L. Shumway, Sacramento, and George J. Marder, Washington staffer.

Marder, who had been on the campaign trail with Kennedy, flew from Los Angeles to New York to join a UPI contingent assigned to the final rites for Kennedy.

Scores of staff men from New York and Washington, including Louis Cassels, UPI Religion Editor and a Senior Editor, helped cover and report the services at St. Patrick's Cathedral, the historic train ride to Washington, and the interment at Arlington Cemetery.

The Editors

Contents

LYING IN STATE—Friday, June 7, 1968

FUNERAL AND BURIAL—Saturday, June 8, 1968

THE NATION MEDITATES—Sunday, June 9, 1968

PRELUDE
TO A
TRAGEDY...

Tuesday, June 4, 1968

Kennedy Wins

New York Senator's victories in California and South Dakota primaries put him ahead of McCarthy in delegate strength.

by De Van L. Shumway

LOS ANGELES (UPI) . . . Senator Robert F. Kennedy's campaign for the Democratic Presidential nomination achieved its brightest victories today.

The New York Democrat, in winning both the California and South Dakota primaries, moved into position to challenge Vice-President Hubert H. Humphrey for the nomination in Chicago in August. Kennedy's victory gave him 172 of California's 174 delegate votes, the biggest primary prize in the nation. Coupled with 24 delegates Kennedy picked up in the South Dakota primary, the Senator now has 393½ convention votes to 258 for Senator Eugene J. McCarthy and 561½ for Humphrey.

The twin wins by Kennedy gave him a record of five victories against a lone loss in the 1968 primary battles with McCarthy.

In a midnight speech, Kennedy claimed victory over McCarthy in the California primary and expressed his thanks to his supporters in a tumultuous gathering in the Embassy room of the Ambassador Hotel on Wilshire Boulevard.

In his talk he deplored the divisions and the violence in the United States. Then Kennedy flashed a V-for-Victory sign and stepped from the podium.

Moments later he lay dying from an assassin's bullet.

13

Standing by his wife Ethel, Robert F. Kennedy flashed the V-for-Victory sign to his campaign workers moments before he was struck down by an assassin's bullet.

Last Speech

"I think we can end the division in the United States."

LOS ANGELES (UPI) . . . The last speech made by Robert F. Kennedy to his campaign workers a few minutes before he was shot:

Thank you very much, thank you very much. Thank you very much. I want to take—can you hear this—you can't hear? Can you hear that? That's great. Can we hear from any of this? Can we get something that works? Just one moment. Can you hear on any of these? Can you hear on that?

I want to first express my high regard to Don Drysdale, who pitched his sixth straight shut-out tonight and I hope that we have as good fortune in our campaign.

Could I express my appreciation to a number of people first? To Jesse Unruh for all that he did, and I express my appreciation to him for his friendship and his help during this campaign and for his continued perseverence and his effort and for all of those who have been associated with him. I'll always be very grateful.

And if I could also express my appreciation to a number of other people, if you'd just bear with me for a moment—I'd like to express my appreciation to Steve Smith, who was ruthless but has been effective and I just want to say how much—how grateful I am to him, to his wife, my sister Jean, to my sister Pat, and to my mother and all of those other Kennedys.

I want to express my gratitude to my dog Freckles who's been relying and I don't care what they—as Franklin Roosevelt said—I don't care what they say about me but when they start to attack my dog. I'm not doing this in the order of importance but I also want to thank my wife Ethel. And her patience during this whole effort was fantastic.

Thank you very much. Freckles is going home to bed. He thought very early that we were going to win so he retired.

I also want to thank Tom—point out Tom Reese who is here and supported us. I want to thank a number of other people if I may. All of those of you who worked so hard in this campaign. All of the 'students who worked across this state. The members of my delegation, our delegation, who also worked so diligently and with such unselfishness across the state on my behalf and on behalf of this cause that we're involved in. I want to thank Cesar Chavez, who was here a little earlier. And Burt Krona who also worked with him and all of those Mexican Americans who were supporters of mine.

And Dolores Balante, who is an old friend of mine and has worked with the union. Thank her and tell her how much I appreciate her coming tonight. We have certain obligations and responsibilities to our fellow citizens which we talked about during the course of this campaign and I want to make it clear that if I'm elected President of the United States with your help I intend to keep it up.

I want to also thank all my friends in the black community who made such an effort in this campaign. With such a high percentage voting today I think it really made a major difference for me. I want to express my appreciation to them.

To my old friend, if I may, to Rafer Johnson who is here. And to Rosie Grier who said that he'd take care of anybody who didn't vote for me. In a kind way because that's what we are. Smile pretty.

And I want to if I may to just take a moment more of your time to express my appreciation to Paul Shrake, who—from the UAW—who worked so hard and all the other members of the labor organizations and members of the labor unions. I am very grateful both to him for what he's done and the effort that he's made on behalf of the working man here in the state of California. I'm very, very appreciative.

I'm very grateful for the votes that I received in the poll that all of you worked for in behalf of the agricultural areas of the state as well as in the city. I think it indicates quite clearly as well as in the suburbs— I think it indicates quite clearly what we could do here in the United States.

The vote here in the state of California, the vote in the state of South Dakota, here is the most urban state of any of the states in our union. South Dakota the most rural state of any of the states in our union, able to win them both. I think that we can end the division within the United States. What I think is—What I think is quite clear is that we can work together in the last analysis and that what has been going on in the United States over the period of the last three years, the division, the violence, the disenchantment with our society, the division whether it's between black and white, between the poor and the more affluent or between age groups or over the war in Vietnam, that we can start to work together. We are a great country and selfish country and a compassionate

17

country. And I intend to make that my basis for running in the period of the next few months.

Ladies and gentlemen, if I can just take a moment more of your time because everybody must be dying from the heat. But what I think all of the primaries have indicated—if I can just take a minute or two minutes more of your time—what all of these primaries have indicated and all of the party caucuses have indicated, whether they occurred in Colorado or Idaho or Iowa, wherever they occurred, it was the people in the Democratic party and the people in the United States want a change. And that change can come about only if they—those who are delegates in Chicago—recognize the importance of what has happened here in the state of California, what has happened in South Dakota, what happened in New Hampshire, what happened across the rest of this country.

The country wants to move in a different direction. We want to deal with our own problems within our own country and we want peace in Vietnam.

I congratulate Senator McCarthy and those who have been associated with him in their efforts that they have started in New Hampshire and carried through to the primary here in the state of California. The fact is that all of us are involved in this great effort and it's a great effort. And it's a great effort not on behalf of the Democratic Party, it's a great effort on the part of the United States, on behalf of our own people, on behalf of mankind all around the globe and the next generation.

And I would hope—I would hope now that the California primary is finished, now that the primary is over, that we can now concentrate on having a dialogue or a debate I hope between the Vice President and perhaps myself on what direction we want to go in the United States.

What we're going to do in the rural areas of this country, what we're going to do for those who still suffer in the United States from hunger. What we're going to do around the rest of the globe and whether we're going to continue the policies which have been so unsuccessful in Vietnam of American troops and American Marines carrying the major burden of that conflict. I do want to and I think we should move in a different direction. Thank you.

So I thank all of you who made all this possible. All of the effort that you made and all of the people whose names I haven't mentioned but who made all the work at the precinct level, who got out to vote, who did all of the efforts and brought forth all of the effort that's required.

I was a campaign manager eight years ago. I know what a difference that kind of effort and that kind of commitment made. I thank all of you.

Mayor Yorty has just sent me a message that we've been here too long already. So my thanks to all of you and on to Chicago and let's win there.

18

SHOOTING

Wednesday, June 5, 1968

Triumphant Victor—
Tragic Victim

When he should have been relishing sweet victory, Robert Kennedy lay dying on a cold kitchen floor.

by Jack V. Fox

LOS ANGELES (UPI) . . . A bullet cut down Senator Robert F. Kennedy at the height of the greatest triumph of his political career. Moments before the bullet pierced his skull, the tousle-haired senator had claimed victory in California's Democratic Presidential primary.

The tragedy was stunning in its suddenness and unreality.

Kennedy had campaigned to the point of exhaustion to win 172 California delegate votes to the Democratic convention in Chicago. As returns showed him pulling ahead of his opponent, Senator Eugene McCarthy, the smiling Kennedy left his suite in Los Angeles' Ambassador Hotel to speak to supporters massed before television cameras in the hotel's Embassy ballroom. Several thousand were in the crowd that cheered the Senator as he spoke of victory.

"What I think is quite clear is that we can work together in the last analysis and that what has been going on in the United States over the period of the last three years, the division, the violence, the disenchantment with our society, the division whether it's between black and white, between the poor and the more affluent or between age groups or over the war in Vietnam that we can start to work together."

He ended, ". . . on to Chicago and let's win there."

Then Kennedy left the podium and began pushing his way through

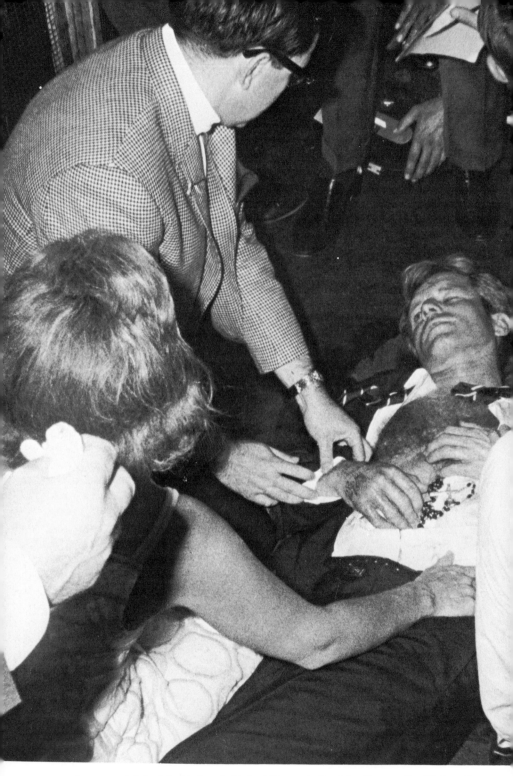

A rosary clutched in his hand, Robert Kennedy lies bleeding on the kitchen floor of the Ambassador Hotel.

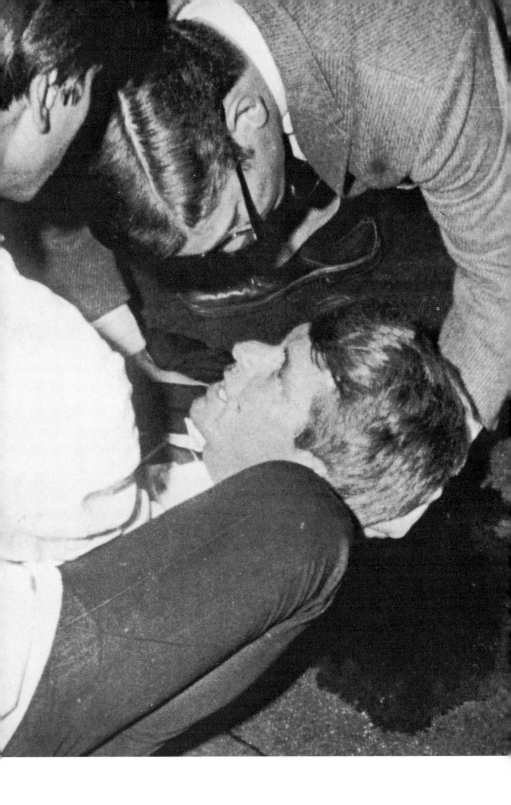

handshaking supporters. With him were a number of aides, including Roosevelt Grier, 300-pound Los Angeles Rams football tackle; Rafer Johnson, former Olympic decathlon champion; and Bill Barry, a former FBI man who had protected Kennedy physically during campaigns.

They headed into a corridor leading to a hotel kitchen, where they planned to get a freight elevator and go back up to their suite. Kennedy was shaking hands with a young busboy near a row of refrigerators when shots began ringing out "like a string of Chinese firecrackers." The time was 12:15 a.m. Pacific daylight time.

From that point eyewitness accounts varied.

Martin Patrusky, 28, a waiter at the Ambassador, said:

"The guy who shot him came out of the corner near the ice machine where Kennedy was standing. He had a kind of funny smile on his face and one hand was in front of the other.

"Then I saw him raise his hands. I didn't know this thing was real until I saw Kennedy sliding down in front of the ice machine. One of the (waiter) captains grabbed the guy by the neck. The guy was waving the gun and a couple more shots went off. I saw two other people fall.

"Everyone was shouting 'Grab the gun.' Then one of the football players (Grier) and one of the other captains grabbed the guy and started pushing him to the floor. I looked back at Kennedy. He was saying, 'Please don't move me.'"

Los Angeles *Times* photographer-reporter Boris Yaro was standing a few feet away.

"Kennedy backed up against the kitchen freezers as the gunman fired at him at point-blank range," he said. "He cringed and threw his hands up over his face. I turned around and saw Kennedy lying on the floor. Blood seemed to be pouring out of a wound in his head or ear."

Karl Uecker, assistant maître d'hôtel at the Ambassador, said he saw the man standing on a three-foot-high steel kitchen table.

In the midst of the confusion Grier and other Kennedy aides rushed the gunman and began wrestling the weapon from him. The man struggled wildly until Grier finally subdued him and sat on him on the floor while others grabbed his gun and held back the crowds. Dozens of police arrived and dragged the gunman from the angry crowd that tore at his head and shouted, "Kill him, kill him."

The swarthy-skinned, bushy-haired young man refused to give his identity to police or talk about the shooting. He was arraigned as "John Doe," and charged with six counts of assault with intent to commit murder. Bail was set at $250,000. Later, Los Angeles Mayor Samuel W. Yorty identified the gunman as Sirhan Bishara Sirhan, 24, a Jordanian immigrant, who was born in Jerusalem when it was an Arab city and came

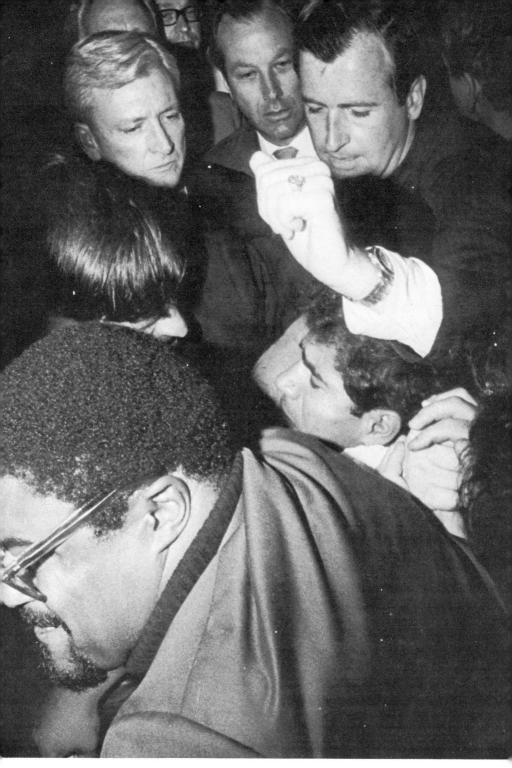

Crowd seizes gunman and forces his weapon from him.

to the United States in 1957. The man had four $100 bills in his possession and a newspaper article critical of Kennedy.

For a few minutes after the shooting the people jammed in the Embassy room had no idea what had happened. Then shouts for a doctor went out over the public address system and the word spread: "Bobby's been shot!"

Pandemonium broke out. Pretty "Kennedy girls" in white blouses and navy blue skirts collapsed, sobbing. One girl ran wildly about the room, tears streaming down her cheeks, shouting over and over, "Oh, he's been shot." A chic matron raised her fist to the ceiling, cried, "No, no!" and then sagged sobbing where she stood.

Kennedy aides sealed off the kitchen and one of them rushed to the microphone in the Embassy room and called out, "Is there a doctor here? We need a doctor." Another Kennedy aide asked all persons to leave the Embassy room, and then cried "We need more doctors."

Police arrived in swarms and urged all to leave the room. Then Stephen Smith, the Senator's brother-in-law, sprang to the podium and shouted, "Please leave. We don't know what has happened."

Gradually and reluctantly most of the crowd except newsmen left the ballroom, without knowing of the capture of the gunman.

In the kitchen, Kennedy lay in a pool of blood, clutching a rosary in his hand. His wife Ethel, unhurt, knelt beside him, whispering to him and trying to console him, just as Jacqueline Kennedy had bent over her husband in a convertible in Dallas in November, 1963. When crowds shoved too close to the Senator, Mrs. Kennedy pushed them away.

"Get back, all of you!" she said. "Get out! Please get out! For God's sake, give him room to breathe!"

In addition to the Senator, five other persons lay wounded by the gunman's bullets. They were Paul Schrade, a United Auto Workers official; William Weisel of the American Broadcasting Company; Ira Goldstein, a Continental News Service reporter; Mrs. Elizabeth Evans of Saugus, Calif.; and Irwin Stroll of Los Angeles.

To the people in the room, it seemed like an interminable time before an ambulance arrived. Mrs. Kennedy at first resisted aid by the ambulance attendants, not realizing who they were. As the Senator was lifted up on a stretcher, he moaned: "Oh no, please don't." Then the wounded man and his wife entered the ambulance and were taken to the Central Receiving Hospital, where Kennedy received the last rites of the Roman Catholic Church.

The Senator was first thought dead at Central Receiving Hospital. The examining physician, Dr. Vasilius Bazilauskas, slapped his face and then listened with a stethoscope. When he heard a heartbeat, he motioned to

Mrs. Kennedy, who listened and then whispered, "Thank God."

Kennedy was transferred to the Good Samaritan Hospital, where an operation to save his life began about 2:45 a.m. Pacific daylight time (5:45 a.m. Eastern daylight time). The operation lasted more than three hours. Shortly afterward, Press Secretary Frank Mankiewicz emerged from the hospital and read a statement. He said the doctors reported Kennedy's condition as "extremely critical."

"The vital signs remain about as they were except he is now breathing on his own which he was not prior to surgery. All but one fragment of the bullet has been removed from the head injury. There is still one bullet apparently somewhere in the back of his neck although this is not regarded as a major problem.

"Senator Kennedy lost a considerable amount of blood as a result of the bullet which entered and passed through the mastoid bone on the right side of his head and some of the fragments of bullet and bone went toward the brain stem.

"In addition to the damage done by the bullet, there may have been impairment of the blood supply to the mid-brain which doctors say controls or at least governs certain vital signs including the eye track, the level of consciousness and, indirectly, the talking processes.

"The doctors said the next 12 to 36 hours will be a very critical period. His condition is listed as extremely critical."

As the day wore on, the medical bulletins became more pessimistic and the prognosis for the Senator's recovery gloomier. One of the physicians who assisted in the operation, Dr. Henry Cuneo, was reported as saying that several major arteries were severed and Kennedy's brain suffered great loss of blood and oxygen as well as several blood clots. Cuneo also said that the Senator suffered injuries to the spinal cord. It is unlikely, he said, that the 42-year-old Kennedy "will be able to recover fully . . . and doubtful that he could live."

"Is Everybody Okay?"

LOS ANGELES (UPI) . . . In some of his last words before lapsing into unconsciousness, Senator Kennedy showed concern for his staff, according to 21-year-old eyewitness Paul Grieco.

"Is everybody okay? Is Paul all right?" Kennedy asked. He was referring to Paul Schrade, a union official who suffered a scalp wound in the shooting. Schrade was a few steps behind the Senator at the shooting.

Police haul swarthy-skinned assailant off to jail.

"I told him everybody was okay and you're going to be okay — just lie still" said Grieco. "Then I held his head because I thought he shouldn't be lying down like that. I thought he would bleed less if I held his head up a little."

A Woodbury College senior, Grieco was among the first to extend aid to Kennedy after the Senator was shot down in the Ambassador Hotel. He held Kennedy's bleeding head in his hands until an ambulance crew arrived.

Grieco, of Ontario, Calif., said Kennedy "was at the height of his consciousness" when he expressed concern for the others.

"He didn't seem to be in too much pain. Although I could see the wound in his head clearly, he wasn't bleeding a great deal," Grieco recalled. "All I could think of was trying to help the man and keep people back as much as I could."

Grieco said the gun "sounded like a kid's cap gun going off very fast. The next thing I knew I was by Kennedy's side trying to help."

Grieco, employed as a part-time bookkeeper with a Los Angeles construction firm while going to college, said he and a friend decided to "look in at the party in the hotel." Grieco said he is a Republican.

En Route to the Hospital

LOS ANGELES (UPI) . . . For one brief moment, Ethel Kennedy gave way to hysteria during the terrible morning of June 5, 1968, and fought the ambulance attendant who was trying to get her husband out of the hotel and to the hospital.

She was sitting beside her husband, rubbing ice on his forehead, when the ambulance arrived, said attendant Max Behrman. "I knelt down but she fought me away — she wouldn't let me touch him.

"I said, 'What do you want an ambulance for then?'

"She said, 'I want to get him to a hospital.'

"I said that was what I was there for.

"We got him on a stretcher but as we did, he said, 'Please don't! Please don't! Please don't lift me.'

"We got him down to the ambulance on a stretcher, but on the way Mrs. Kennedy kept pulling back on the stretcher saying she didn't want it going too fast — that we were hurting him," Behrman said.

"We got him into the ambulance. I wanted a little information for my book. She took it out of my hand and threw it into the lot of the hotel.

"From what I could see, he needed a bandage on his head—at the right ear where one bullet wound was. And I had to give him oxygen which he needed very badly."

According to Warren Rogers, LOOK correspondent who accompanied Mrs. Kennedy in the ambulance, she kept pleading with the attendants to be gentle. She sat in the back near her husband, while Rogers and a Kennedy aide sat up front. At one point Mrs. Kennedy signaled to Rogers that her husband couldn't breathe. Rogers shouted to the attendant sitting near the Senator, and he reached over and produced a small, clear-plastic breathing mask. "Roughly," Rogers wrote, "he stretched the elastic attached to it over Kennedy's head, scraping the bullet wound that gaped behind his right ear. Ethel shivered with horror."

Refused Protection

LOS ANGELES (UPI) . . . Police Chief Thomas Reddin said that Senator Robert F. Kennedy was offered a security guard several times during his visit to the city, but refused it.

"We were asked to leave the party alone," the chief told a news conference at the Central Police Building in downtown Los Angeles.

But Kennedy's campaign press secretary, Frank Mankiewicz, claimed that the protection of the Los Angeles police department had not been offered to the Senator and therefore could not have been refused.

The Wounded

Five persons wounded along with Senator Kennedy by the gunman's shots Wednesday morning had all been treated and were recuperating by Wednesday night.

Paul Schrade, 43, of Los Angeles, United Auto Workers Regional Director, was in satisfactory condition at Kaiser Foundation Hospital, after undergoing a two-hour operation for removal of bullet fragments from his skull. The bullet did not penetrate his brain.

William Weisel, 30, of Washington, D.C., an American Broadcasting Company Associate News Director, was also in satisfactory condition at Kaiser Foundation Hospital, where he underwent surgery for removal of a bullet in his abdomen.

Ira Goldstein, 19, of Encino, Calif., a Continental News Service re-

31

porter, was treated at Encino Hospital for a bullet wound received in his left thigh.

Mrs. Elizabeth Evans, of Saugus, Calif., a Kennedy supporter, was in good condition at Huntington Memorial Hospital, where she was treated for a scalp wound.

Irwin Stroll, 17, of Los Angeles, was in good condition at Midway Hospital, where he was treated for a wound in the lower left leg.

Wounded by one of eight gunshots, Mrs. Elizabeth Evans holds bleeding head.
Five persons were hit in addition to Kennedy.

Broadcast on the Scene

"...The shock is so great.
My mouth is dry..."

Seconds before Senator Kennedy was shot, Mutual Broadcasting System correspondent Andrew West interviewed him amidst his jubilant supporters. As the interview ended, West followed Kennedy through a hallway into the hotel kitchen. There he turned his tape recorder back on just as crowds began to scream that Kennedy had been shot. In a highly emotional voice, West continued to report and describe the scene. At the same time he shouted directions to bystanders, ordering them to disarm the assailant and to shut the doors to the kitchen. Here is the text of the tape that was later broadcast, copyrighted by station KRKD and the Mutual Broadcasting System:

"Senator Kennedy has been shot . . . Senator Kennedy has been shot . . . is that possible, is that possible? It is possible, ladies and gentlemen. It is possible. He has. Not only Senator Kennedy . . . Oh, my God . . . Senator Kennedy has been shot and another man . . a Kennedy campaign manager . . and possibly shot in the head. I am right here and Rafer Johnson has hold of the man who apparently has fired the shot. He has fired the shot . . . He still has the gun, the gun is pointed at me right this moment. I hope they can get the gun out of his hand. Be very careful. Get the gun . . . Get the gun . . . Get the gun . . . Stay away from the gun . . . Stay away from the gun.

"His hand is frozen . . . Get his thumb . . . Get his thumb . . . Get his thumb . . Get his thumb . . . Get his thumb. Take a hold of his thumb . . . and break it if you have to . . . Get his thumb. Get away from the barrel. Get away from the barrel, man. Look out for the gun. OK . . . all right. That's it Rafer, get it. Get the gun Rafer. OK now hold on to the gun. Hold on to him. Hold on to him.

"Ladies and gentlemen they have the gun away from the man. In this . . . they've got the gun. I can't see the man. I can't see who it is. Senator

Kennedy right now is on the ground. He has been shot. This is a . . . this is . . . what is it? Wait a minute. Hold him . . . hold him. Hold him. We don't want another Oswald. Hold him, Rafer. We don't want another Oswald. Hold him, Rafer. Keep people away from him. Keep people away from him. All right, ladies and gentlemen. This is a . . . make room, make room, make room, make room, make room. The Senator is on the ground. He's bleeding profusely . . . from apparently . . . clear back . . . apparently the Senator has been shot from the frontal area. We can't see exactly where the Senator has been shot. But come on, push back, grab a hold of me, grab hold of me and let's pull back. That's it. Come on. Get hold of my arms. Let's pull back. Let's pull back. All right. They . . . the Senator is now . . . the ambulance has been called for and the ambulance is bringing the ambulance in this entrance. And this is a terrible thing. It's reminiscent of the valley the other day when the Senator was out there and somebody hit him in the head with a rock. And people couldn't believe it at that time. But it is a fact.

"Keep room. Ethel Kennedy is standing by. She is calm. She's raising her hand high to motion people back. She is attempting to get calm. A woman with a tremendous amount of presence. A tremendous amount of presence. It's impossible to believe. It's impossible to believe. There's a certain amount of fanaticism here now . . . as this has occurred no one . . . we're trying to run everybody back. Clear the area. Clear the area. Right at this moment . . . the Senator apparently . . . we can't see if he is still conscious or not. Can you see if he is conscious?"

Observer—"What?"

West—"Can you see if he is conscious?"

Observer—"I don't know . . . no, no . . . he is half conscious."

West—"He is half conscious, and ladies, we can't see . . . ladies and gentlemen . . . one of the men, apparently a Kennedy supporter, is going berserk. Come on . . . come on . . . out, out, out. Is there some way to close these doors, Jess? Is there any doors here? Out through the . . . out through the exit . . . let's go. Out we go . . . unbelievable situation. They're clearing the halls.

"One man has blood on himself. We're walking down the corridors here. Repetition in my speech . . . I have no alternative. The shock is so great. My mouth is dry. I can only say that here in the kitchen of the Ambassador Hotel . . . the back entrance . . . from the podium . . . in the Press Room. The Senator walked out the back. I was directly behind him. You heard a balloon go off and a shot. You didn't really realize that the shot was a shot. Screams went up . . . Two men were on the ground . . . both bleeding profusely. One of them was Senator Robert Kennedy. At this moment, we are stunned. We are shaking as is everyone else. In this kitchen corridor at the Ambassador Hotel in Los Angeles . . . they're blocking off the entrance now. Supposedly to make room for the ambulance. That's all we can report at this moment. I do not know if the Senator is dead or if he is alive. We do not know the name of the gentleman concerned. This is Andrew West, Mutual News, Los Angeles."

Accused Assassin: A Pistol, A Diary, Identification

"Kennedy has to be assassinated before June 5, 1968."

by Paul R. Jeschke

LOS ANGELES (UPI) . . . The man who allegedly shot Senator Robert F. Kennedy and wounded five others was identified about three hours after the shooting as Sirhan Bishara Sirhan, a Jordanian immigrant who came to the United States from Arab Jerusalem in 1957. Los Angeles Mayor Sam Yorty said the man had been identified by his brother, who was believed to have owned the weapon involved in the shooting.

The gunman had emptied eight shots from a .22-caliber revolver at Kennedy from a distance of three feet. Seconds after the shooting, Kennedy aides jumped him and forced the gun from his hands. He refused to identify himself and was arraigned officially as "John Doe."

Sirhan lived in nearby Pasadena with his mother and two brothers, Adel and Munir (Joe) Sirhan. The gun supposedly belonged to Munir. Police questioned both brothers extensively and later released them without charge.

Mayor Yorty said that Sirhan had four $100 bills in his possession and a newspaper clipping critical of Kennedy. The clipping suggested that Kennedy was inconsistent in opposing the Vietnam War while supporting U.S. aid to Israel to match the Soviet building of military strength in Arab states.

In addition, the mayor said, a diary, handwritten in a spiral notebook, was seized at the suspect's home. Yorty said an entry of May 18 read, "Kennedy has to be assassinated before June 5, 1968." June 5 was the date

37

of the first anniversary of the six-day-war between Israel and the Arab states in 1967. The diary was also peppered with criticisms of Kennedy and with sentiments backing the Arab side in the Middle East war with Israel. In addition, it contained many pro-communist and anti-American sentiments, according to Yorty.

The swarthy, bushy-haired suspect was being held under maximum security in Los Angeles County jail after being whisked away at 7 a.m. to a secret arraignment, where he was charged with six counts of assault with intent to commit murder. Bail was set at $250,000. Some 40 police guards witnessed the proceedings along with the district attorney and a representative of the public defender's office.

Justice Department records in Washington showed Sirhan was one of a family of eight Jordanians admitted to the United States for permanent residence. None was ever naturalized. Sirhan and six other members of the family arrived at New York on Jan. 12, 1957, a few months after the Suez crisis, one of the major outbreaks in the series of conflicts between Israel and the Arab nations. The family consisted of a father, mother, five sons, and one daughter. The father has returned to the Middle East and Sirhan's sister is dead.

Los Angeles Police Chief Thomas Reddin said Sirhan was calm under questioning and wanted to talk about everything except the shooting.

"He almost appeared to be the calmest man in the room," Reddin said.

"I spoke with him for about 15 minutes and he sounds well educated, speaks good English and is a good conversationalist.

"We talked about many things. He was very relaxed and wanted to talk about just about everything except the events last night.

"If I were to judge him strictly on the basis of our conversation, and that were the only basis, I would say he was a gentleman."

The curious gather at home of accused assassin, Sirhan Bishara Sirhan, in Pasadena, Calif.

As Others Saw Sirhan

"All I know is that he is a nice
kid. That's all I know."

by Edward O'Connor

LOS ANGELES (UPI) . . . Sirhan Bishara Sirhan, the swarthy, 24-year-old immigrant arrested for the shooting of Senator Robert F. Kennedy, cared deeply about money, his personal rights, and the cause of the Arabs in the Middle East war.

That was the picture that emerged Wednesday from friends, neighbors, relatives, and former employers of the unemployed man who once worked as an exercise boy at a race track and a stock boy in a health food store.

"He was a hard worker—honest and good hearted—but nonetheless a fanatic when it came to discussions of religion and politics," said Mrs. Elsie Boyko, a former co-worker at the Organic Health Food store in Pasadena, about a block and a half from the middle-class neighborhood where Sirhan lived.

"Never would I think there was any violence in him," said Mrs. Boyko, who believed Sirhan was "either Egyptian or Arabian."

"We all called him Sol around the store, everyone did," she said.

The owner of the store, John H. Weidner Jr., said Sirhan worked for him for about seven months before quitting last March after an argument over money.

"I think he did it because he thought he was doing something for his country, but not necessarily the United States," Weidner said.

Weidner said Sirhan "told me that when he was a child, he saw members of his family killed by Jews and he had to flee Jordan when he was a child. He was not a citizen and didn't like the United States. You had to be careful not to walk on his feet. He wanted you to respect him intellectually. He was a man who said 'I'm going to have my rights.'"

A high school classmate now living in Mexico City remembers that, though Sirhan had a five o'clock shadow, he was fastidious about always wearing a clean white shirt. When police arrested Sirhan early Wednesday morning he was wearing blue jeans and a rumpled colored shirt.

The high school classmate also recalled that Sirhan was a shy, sensitive lad. "Sirhan wouldn't hurt a fly," she said.

Alvin Clark, 40, a neighbor, said Sirhan "hated Kennedy because he hated everyone with money."

Although Sirhan apparently has not worked recently, Clark said, he received a $1,100 settlement last month from a head injury suffered when he was thrown from a horse.

Records of the California Horse Racing Board indicated Sirhan had a license in 1966 as a "hot walker" and "exercise boy" and failed to renew the license in 1967 or 1968.

Olive Blakesley, another neighbor, described Sirhan as a "fine boy, good looking, polite, clean, willing to help, never in any trouble . . . never found anything wrong with him."

And neighbor Brandon Lamont said the Sirhans were a "quiet family and kept to themselves."

"I saw Sirhan about two days ago," Lamont said. "I said 'Hello' to him, 'How are you?' but that's about the only conversation we had."

Although some neighbors thought Sirhan's mother had died recently, a brother told newsmen she was still alive.

"I really have no idea about this man," the brother told newsmen. "I mean this is really something that shook me up. That my brother would do such a thing. All I know is that he is a nice kid. That's all I know."

Stiff Security for Suspect

"After Dallas, nobody is going to get within a thousand feet of him."

by Vernon Scott

LOS ANGELES (UPI) . . . With the memory of Lee Harvey Oswald and Jack Ruby in mind, Los Angeles police kept tight security around Sirhan Sirhan, accused gunman in the shooting of Robert Kennedy. When asked by newsmen whether they could interview the prisoner, Police Chief Thomas Reddin replied, "After Dallas, nobody is going to get within a thousand feet of him."

At a press conference held before the identity of the suspect was established, newsmen were frisked for weapons—for the first time in the memory of veteran reporters.

After the prisoner had been identified and taken to the county jail, a Justice Department spokesman said Attorney General Ramsey Clark had telephoned Reddin three times to insist on security for Sirhan.

"The security is so tight there that only the sheriff and a few guards know where he is," Reddin said. "Even I don't know exactly where he is."

Reddin said Sirhan broke a finger and sprained an ankle in the struggle that broke out moments after the shots were fired. The injuries were minor, Reddin said, adding, "We'll take the treatment to the man and not the man to the treatment."

Officials also voiced concern that the accused receive a fair trial, particularly in light of Mayor Sam Yorty's revelations about Sirhan's diary. Reddin would not comment on the mayor's disclosure of the notebook with the implied threat that "Kennedy has to be assassinated before June 5, 1968." He said, however, that his men were no longer questioning Sirhan because "an interview may damage the case."

Officials of the Southern California chapter of the American Civil Liberties Union (ACLU) said Yorty's revelation was "to be regretted" and could prejudice Sirhan's chance for a fair trial.

A. L. Wirin, Chief ACLU counsel, said, "With the exception of the statement attributed to Mayor Yorty, the response of public officials and the press has been commendable."

Wirin said he did not criticize newspapers, television, and radio for using Yorty's statement, even if it prejudices Sirhan's case.

"Our objection is to the statement by the public official," he said.

Eason Monroe, executive director of the chapter, said the ACLU would help Sirhan obtain a private lawyer of his own choice. But he said the ACLU "does not intend to represent this man. There is no constitutional right to assassinate."

Monroe said the ACLU entered the case because Sirhan "must be provided all the constitutional rights to a fair trial, effective counsel, and due process."

Question of Conspiracy

WASHINGTON (UPI) . . . Attorney General Ramsey Clark said there is "no evidence of a conspiracy at this moment" in the shooting of Senator Robert F. Kennedy.

Clark told a news conference in the Justice Department auditorium that Kennedy used as an office when he was Attorney General that information so far indicates the shooting was "just an individual act."

Clark earlier had ordered an FBI investigation of the shooting. He also ordered James P. McShane, Chief U.S. Marshal, to the Kennedy home in suburban Virginia.

Clark told reporters the FBI "is working side by side with the Los Angeles Police Department."

"I have ordered them to make a full and thorough investigation of every aspect of this crime," he added.

Clark, his voice breaking with emotion, recalled how he had worked with Kennedy in the very office where he was meeting with reporters. He was an Assistant Attorney General at the time.

Clark said he was advised of the shooting about 3:30 a.m. Eastern daylight time—shortly after it happened—and he had since been in frequent touch about it with President Johnson, FBI Director J. Edgar Hoover, and other members of the FBI, the Secret Service, and the chief of police of Los Angeles.

Ethel Didn't Cry Either

They are made of solid stuff, the Kennedy women. They have to be. Fate seems to move from one to another and say, "Now it's your turn. Now it's your husband."

by Jack V. Fox

LOS ANGELES (UPI) . . . Awaiting the birth of her 11th child in January, Ethel Skakel Kennedy bent over her husband, lying in a pool of blood on the floor in the awful glare of television lights, and murmured to him. It was heartbreakingly reminiscent of another slim girl bending over a stricken husband in a convertible in Dallas.

When Robert Kennedy moaned as they carried him to the ambulance on a stretcher and cried, "Oh, no, don't," it was too much. She screamed at the ambulance attendant and hit at his face as he tried to put a bandage on the head wound. Then she found control.

At Central Receiving Hospital, she watched a doctor slap her husband's face, trying to revive a spark through pain. She took the stethoscope proffered by the doctor and heard for herself the beat of Robert Kennedy's heart.

She followed in the ambulance to Good Samaritan Hospital and waited in a private lounge while surgeons for three hours removed fragments from the interior of the stricken man's skull. Her friend Claudine Longet, the wife of singer Andy Williams, said she never once wept.

Afterward she talked with John Glenn, and the astronaut walked grimly from the hospital to gather up six of the Kennedy brood who had come to Los Angeles to be with their so-often-absent parents and to take them back to Hickory Hill.

44

Then the clan gathered around Ethel. Jean Smith, Bobby's sister, stayed close by her side. Patricia, the divorced wife of actor Peter Lawford, came to the hospital and then left, leaning on a companion for support.

From across a continent, Jacqueline Kennedy boarded a private plane and flew to the side of the man who had stood by her side at a grave in Arlington Cemetery. From the plane she drove in a white limousine to the hospital.

At the hospital also was Ted, the youngest of the Kennedy boys. His wife, too, had known fear for a husband's life. Senator Edward Kennedy suffered a broken back when a private plane crashed in Southampton, Mass., in June, 1964, but he pulled through.

In Hyannis Port, Mass., Mrs. Rose Kennedy, the mother, heard about Bobby shortly after she rose to attend 7 a.m. mass. She had lost her oldest son, Joe, in World War II and then Jack. Her husband, the tough old father of the clan, sat in a wheelchair in Hyannis, victim of a stroke a few years ago. Another of her children, Rosemary, had been mentally retarded since birth. And a daughter, Kathleen, died in a plane crash in France.

Now it was Ethel's turn.

In the past weeks she had been flip and happy campaigning with her husband, riding at his side in the motorcade through idolatrous crowds. She looked anxious at times when it appeared they would pull him from the car, but by Tuesday night it was all over. Bobby had won in California and they could go back with the kids to Hickory Hill for a few days.

Then they walked out together toward an elevator, where a man with a gun was waiting.

In her 40 years of life, she has known tragedies that would destroy a lesser person.

Ethel Kennedy drew on a seemingly infinite reservoir of strength in her moment of shock and sorrow. She had been campaigning alongside her husband since he entered the Presidential race in March, asking no special treatment even though she is expecting her 11th child. She was at his side when he was shot, rode with him to the hospital, and remained on vigil through his more than three hours of brain surgery. She was "amazingly calm" and "extremely brave," according to Msgr. Joseph J. Truxaw, who said mass and served communion in the Good Samaritan Hospital chapel for members of the family.

This was not her first taste of tragedy and suffering. In 1955, both her parents, Mr. and Mrs. George Skakel, were killed in a private airplane crash. A plane crash also claimed the life of her brother, George Jr., in 1966. Less than a year later, her brother's widow choked to death on a piece of meat at the dinner table.

A member of the Kennedy clan by marriage, Ethel always epitomized the Kennedy trademarks of fighting spirit, courage, and family loyalty.

A sportswoman of considerable ability, she played touch football with the Kennedys, went skiing with them, and was an enthusiastic horse-woman.

She made headlines by falling off a motorcycle in Rome, and falling into the ocean when a boat overturned off Hawaii.

But in Washington, where she had a large circle of close friends, Ethel was known for her compassion for deprived children.

She opened her luxurious home, Hickory Hill at McLean, Va., to them on numerous occasions and organized a three-day telethon in Washington in February to raise funds for poor children.

Ethel had long lived in the shadow of her famous sister-in-law, former First Lady Jacqueline Kennedy. The two never had a particularly warm rapport, although they closed ranks in times of crisis.

She is one of seven children of George Skakel, a multimillionaire who headed the Great Lakes Carbon Corporation. She was born in Chicago and reared in Greenwich, Conn.

While attending the Manhattanville College of the Sacred Heart, she roomed with Jean Kennedy and met Bobby during her freshman year in 1945 on a ski trip to Canada.

They were married in June, 1950, and one of Ethel's announced goals —now achieved—was to surpass her mother-in-law, Mrs. Rose Kennedy, who had nine children.

Her husband was considerably amused when Ethel was tried in 1967, charged with being a horse thief.

Nicholas N. Zemo of the McLean area accused her of stealing a thor-oughbred yearling named Pande. Mrs. Kennedy testified at her trial that the horse was starving, so she took him in to feed him. The horse died soon after she had her groom take it from a chicken coop to the stables on her estate. She was acquitted and Zemo was convicted of cruelty to animals.

Jacqueline: "No! It Can't Have Happened."

For Mrs. John F. Kennedy, the
unbelievable nightmare had come again.

NEW YORK (UPI) . . . A telephone rang in an apartment on New York's
Fifth Avenue, awakening Mrs. Jacqueline Kennedy. It was her sister,
Princess Lee Radziwill, calling from London to tell her that her brother-
in-law had been shot in Los Angeles.

"No! It can't have happened. No! It can't have happened," she cried
in stunned disbelief. "Tell me more."

Several hours later she was driven to Kennedy International Airport
where she met her brother-in-law, Prince Stanislas Radziwill, who flew
in from London. Together they boarded a twin-engine jet owned by the
International Business Machines Corporation. The plane had been made
available to Mrs. Kennedy for her flight to Los Angeles. From the Los
Angeles airport, Mrs. Kennedy drove in a white limousine to the hospital
where Robert Kennedy lay fighting for his life. She wore a white coat and
brown dress and her dark hair streamed down her back.

Mrs. Kennedy had gone to bed several hours before the shooting, after
visiting Kennedy headquarters in New York and learning of Kennedy's
lead over Senator McCarthy.

And Yet Another Son Struck by Violence

News of the shooting shatters
quiet life of the elder Kennedys.

by John McDonough

HYANNIS PORT, MASS. (UPI) . . . A bright sun sparkled on the Kennedy compound as workmen routinely worked on Senator Robert F. Kennedy's house, installing windows, painting and repairing odds and ends. Several small boats bobbed easily at a private pier on Irving Street, which borders the compound.

Mrs. Rose Kennedy, the energetic 77-year-old matriarch of the family, was preparing to go to 7 a.m. mass, as is her daily custom.

Casually, she turned on a television set.

"Senator Kennedy lies in critical condition . . . shot in the brain . . ." the newscaster said.

Mrs. Kennedy was stunned. Once again violence had reached into the family and struck down a son.

Joseph P. Kennedy, who will be 80 in September and has been an invalid since a stroke in 1961, did not know of the Senator's condition. He learned it later, inadvertently overhearing part of a telephone conversation from his youngest son, Senator Edward M. Kennedy, as he gave his mother the details. The elder Kennedy, a former ambassador to Great Britain, wept in his wheelchair when he overheard the conversation. Mrs. Kennedy concealed her sorrow lest her husband become even more upset.

"They took it with remarkable courage," said a source close to the family.

Richard Cardinal Cushing, Roman Catholic Archbishop of Boston and a longtime family friend, called and offered his sympathies. He also said a special mass for the Senator.

Mrs. Kennedy, wearing sunglasses and a shawl over her dress, sat in a front pew at St. Francis Xavier Roman Catholic Church with attorney John Driscoll of Boston, another family friend. Her head was bowed as she left and returned to the compound, which sets on Nantucket Sound, and where the late President, Bobby, and Teddy sailed regularly.

Joseph Kennedy, 15, the New York Senator's oldest son and namesake of an uncle who was an American flying ace before his death in World War II, came from Milton Academy near Boston. The young sophomore stayed about 45 minutes before returning to Boston and then flying with his sister, Kathleen, 16, to the West Coast.

State and local police marshaled traffic away from the compound, which is surrounded by a hedge and unpainted wooden fence.

And the small boats, which have carried—and undoubtedly will carry—Kennedy children onto Nantucket Sound, continued to skip gently as an easy breeze crossed the calm waters.

14-year-old Bobby Jr. cries at the family's Virginia estate as he learns of the shooting of his father. He is comforted by the Rev. Richard McSorley, professor of theology at Georgetown University.

Kennedy Children Learn the News

An untouched football, an unnatural silence reflect stunned sadness of Robert Kennedy's children.

by Helen Thomas

MCLEAN, VA. (UPI) . . . Life seemed to stand still at Hickory Hill, the Robert F. Kennedy estate. A football lay on the grass, its well-worn cover glistening in the early morning dew—a motionless memento of yesterday's fun.

Past it strolled a slim tousle-headed boy. A Roman Catholic priest walked with him, his arm on the youngster's shoulder. They wandered aimlessly, followed by Brumus, the family dog.

Robert Francis Kennedy, 14, was asleep when his father, Senator Robert F. Kennedy, was shot in the head 3,000 miles to the west in Los Angeles. The news had been broken to him after he arose in the early morning. Shortly afterward, the Reverend Richard McSorley, professor of theology at Georgetown University, arrived to console the youngster. Mrs. Dean Markham also came to help at the big, white house.

Bobby Jr., 14, and 14-month-old Douglas Harriman were at home when the tragedy occurred. The six children who had been with their parents in Los Angeles were being flown back to Washington in a special Air Force jet provided by President Johnson. They are David Anthony, 12, Mary Courtney, 11, Michael LeMoyne, 10, Mary Kerry, 8, Christopher George, 4, and Matthew Maxwell Taylor, 3. John Glenn, the astronaut, and his wife were accompanying them.

Joseph P. Kennedy III, 15, was at Milton Academy in Milton, Mass.,

51

when an instructor gently broke the news. He left to go to the Kennedy family compound at Hyannis Port, Mass., to be with his grieving grandparents.

Kathleen Huntington, 16, was at school. Both she and Joseph planned to fly to the West Coast.

A diaper truck arrived at Hickory Hill at mid-morning.

In the afternoon, six members of Kennedy's campaign staff came out to the estate to try to keep young Bobby occupied.

They picked up the football and engaged in a spirited game of touch for a while, as three horses grazed on the lawn nearby.

But their hearts were not in the game. Nothing they could do could break the silence.

Kennedy Clan: Stalked by Tragedy

"I guess the only reason we've survived is that there are too many of us," Robert Kennedy once said. "There are more of us than there is trouble."

WASHINGTON (UPI) . . . For the family of Joseph Patrick Kennedy, violence and agony have been interwoven with brilliant success and wealth. Kennedy and his wife Rose bore nine children. Their third, a girl named Rosemary, was born mentally retarded and has spent much of her life in an institution. The others and their families have been struck time and again by tragedy.

The chain of misfortunes began in 1944 during World War II when the eldest of Kennedy's children, Joseph Jr., was killed after his plane exploded. He had been on a dangerous mission to destroy German submarine pens along the French coast.

Tragedy struck again in May, 1948, when a daughter, Kathleen, died in a plane crash in France. Her husband, too, had been killed four years earlier during the war.

In 1955, Robert Kennedy's parents-in-law, Mr. and Mrs. George Skakel, met death in a plane crash.

In 1961, Joseph P. Kennedy Sr. suffered a stroke and has been an invalid ever since.

In August, 1963, President John F. Kennedy's newborn son, Patrick, died of a lung ailment.

Then, on Nov. 22, 1963, came the assassination of President Kennedy.

Even after that the tragedies continued. Senator Edward M. Kennedy, the Kennedys' youngest son, was in a private plane crash at Southampton,

Mass., in June, 1964. He suffered a back injury but survived.

Robert's brother-in-law, George Skakel, and his closest friend, Dean Markham, died in a plane crash in September, 1966.

And then on June 5, 1968, came the shooting of Robert F. Kennedy himself.

President Appoints Commission on Violence

"Let us, for God's sake,
resolve to live under the law."

WASHINGTON (UPI) . . . With this solemn invocation to a troubled nation, President Johnson Wednesday night dispatched a select nine-member panel on the mission of seeking causes for violence of the sort that struck down Robert F. Kennedy.

In a 7½ minute address on nationwide television and radio, the President said:

"My fellow citizens, we cannot, we just must not, tolerate the sway of violent men among us. We must not permit men who are filled with hatred, and careless of innocent lives, to dominate our streets and fill our homes with fear.

"We cannot sanction the appeal to violence, no matter what its cause and no matter what the grievance from which it sprang . . .

"A great nation can guarantee freedom for its people and the hope of progressive change only under the rule of law. So let us, for God's sake, resolve to live under the law."

To head the special commission, the President chose Dr. Milton S. Eisenhower, president emeritus of The Johns Hopkins University and brother of former President Dwight D. Eisenhower.

Other members are Archbishop Terence Cooke of New York; Albert E. Jenner Jr., a Chicago lawyer who worked for the Warren Commission; Patricia Harris, former Ambassador to Luxembourg; Eric Hoffer, the West Coast longshoreman-philosopher; Senators Philip A. Hart, D-Mich., and Roman Hruska, R-Neb.; Representatives Hale Boggs, D-La., and William M. McCulloch, R-Ohio, and A. Leon Higgenbotham Jr., U.S. District Judge for Eastern Pennsylvania.

55

The President said it would be self-deceptive to ignore the connection between lawlessness and hatred in general and the shooting of Kennedy. Then he added:

"It would be just as wrong, just as self-deceptive, to conclude from this act that our country is sick, that it has lost its sense of balance, its sense of direction and common decency.

"Two hundred million Americans did not strike Robert Kennedy last night any more than they struck John F. Kennedy in 1963 or Martin Luther King in April of this year.

"But those awful events give us ample warning that in a climate of extremism, of disrespect for law, of contempt for the rights of others, violence may bring down the very best among us. A nation that tolerates violence in any form cannot expect to be able to confine it to just minor outbursts."

Johnson said the commission "will look into the causes, the occurrence, and the control of physical violence across this nation, from assassination that is motivated by prejudice and by ideology, and by politics and by insanity, to violence in our cities' streets and even in our homes.

". . . This is a sober time for our great democracy, but we are a strong and a resilient people who can, I hope, learn from our misfortunes, who can heal our wounds, who can build and find progress in public order.

"We can. We must."

Nine Who Will Study Violence

Here are thumbnail sketches of the nine members of President Johnson's Special Commission to Study Violence in America:

Dr. Milton S. Eisenhower, 68, president emeritus of The Johns Hopkins University, Baltimore, Md., and brother of former President Dwight D. Eisenhower. Now residing at the University, he is a former president of Kansas State and Pennsylvania State Universities and has been associated with numerous government offices since the 1920's.

Archbishop Terence Cooke of New York, who succeeded the late Francis Cardinal Spellman as Roman Catholic Prelate for New York. He was the Cardinal's former secretary before he was named Papal Chamberlain and Vice Chancellor of the New York Archdiocese.

Albert E. Jenner Jr., a Chicago lawyer who was on the legal staff of the Warren Commission that investigated the assassination of President John F. Kennedy. He is a former Special Assistant Attorney General of Illinois and former president of the American College of Trial Lawyers.

Patricia Harris, former U.S. Ambassador to Luxembourg, who now is a law professor at Howard University in Washington. A 44-year-old Negro native of Illinois, she once was a lawyer in the Justice Department's Criminal Appeals and Research Section.

Eric Hoffer, a 65-year-old San Francisco longshoreman and self-made philosopher whose nationally televised interview last year prompted President Johnson to invite him to the White House for a mutually satisfying conversation. Hoffer has written three books expressing his views.

Senator Philip A. Hart, D-Mich., a 55-year-old liberal who was elected to the Senate in 1958. He is a leading Senate civil rights advocate and an opponent of stringent controls on firearms sales. He is a former Lieutenant Governor of Michigan and legal adviser to former Governor G. Mennen Williams.

Senator Roman Hruska, R-Neb., a 63-year-old Omaha lawyer first elected to Congress in 1952. He is a firm opponent of the administration's gun control legislative proposals.

Representative Hale Boggs, D-La., the House Democratic Whip and a close friend of the Johnsons. Now 54 years old, he was a member of the Warren Commission that investigated the John F. Kennedy assassination in 1963.

Representative William M. McCulloch, R-Ohio, elected to Congress in 1947, the 66-year-old Piqua, Ohio, resident is the ranking Republican Member of the House Judiciary Committee and is known as one of the most influential civil rights advocates in the House.

A. Leon Higginbotham Jr., 40-year-old Negro U.S. District Judge for Eastern Pennsylvania who was a member of the Federal Trade Commission under President John F. Kennedy.

Los Angeles Police Chief Thomas Reddin shows newsmen the point at which the bullet struck Kennedy. Top, station WPIX-TV in New York broadcast the single word "SHAME" without sound for 2½ hours Wednesday morning.

A Shot Heard Round the World

Shock, shame, and cries of "No, not again," greet news of the shooting of Bobby Kennedy.

by Mike Feinsilber

WASHINGTON (UPI) . . . Heartsick, stunned, tormented anew, the capital prayed Wednesday for the recovery of Senator Robert F. Kennedy from his wounds and for the recovery of America from the torment of violence and assassination.

President Johnson, witness to the slaying of John F. Kennedy in Dallas on Nov. 22, 1963, said "there are no words equal to the horror" of the attempted assassination of his predecessor's brother in Los Angeles.

Johnson, awakened in the White House and told the news by aide Walt W. Rostow at 3:31 a.m., stayed awake, watched the news on television, and dispatched Secret Service agents to protect all major candidates for Presidential nominations and their families—even though he lacked legal authority to do so. He asked Congress to pass a law at once to make such protection a permanent aspect of American political life.

The President conferred by telephone with Senator Edward M. Kennedy, the youngest of the four ill-starred Kennedy brothers, and with Theodore Sorensen, one of Robert Kennedy's advisers.

At the President's side as he received the news, Mrs. Johnson expressed her personal "anguish."

After the long night, the President issued this statement:

"There are no words equal to the horror of this tragedy. Our thoughts and our prayers are with Senator Kennedy, his family and the other victims. All America prays for his recovery. We also pray that divisiveness and violence be driven from the hearts of men everywhere."

The President also conferred with FBI Director J. Edgar Hoover; James Rowley, the Secret Service Director; and Attorney General Ramsey Clark. Adhering to his schedule, he met with the new Ambassador of Senegal and with the National Security Council.

In quick order as the day wore on:

—The Senate Appropriations Committee approved the legislation the President requested. Congress was likely to pass it Thursday.

—Congressmen called for approval of stiff gun control measures, which had been favored by Kennedy. Republicans in the House pressed for immediate approval of anticrime legislation carrying relatively mild gun controls, limited only to pistols.

—Senate Democratic Leader Mike Mansfield proposed creation of a special committee "to find ways and means to cope with violence on the American political scene."

—Kennedy's opponents for the Democratic Presidential nomination, Senator Eugene J. McCarthy and Vice President Hubert H. Humphrey, and the Republican contenders, Richard M. Nixon and Governor Nelson A. Rockefeller of New York, called off politicking.

As word of the shooting spread, Kennedy's friends and his political opponents as well as the man in the street expressed shock and grief and deplored lawlessness.

Mrs. Martin Luther King Jr., who was consoled by the Kennedys when her husband was slain in Memphis, Tenn., April 4, said in a telegram to Mrs. Ethel Kennedy: "I am praying for your husband, who I so much respect, and I am praying for our country in this period of great national tragedy and peril."

At Resurrection City, about 300 marchers knelt on the muddy ground while their leader, the Rev. Ralph David Abernathy, prayed for Kennedy's soul. "God, please look on Senator Kennedy," he said. "If he must follow in the path of his brother, give him peace somewhere."

Representative Sherman Lloyd, R-Utah, said that, in view of the event, the best service the leaders of the Poor People's March could perform now "would be to disband and tell their people to go home" to "put an end to activities which incite passions."

"We the people must look deep into our hearts and ask what we are," said Attorney General Clark. "We will weather this. But we must restore reason and order to our lives."

Senator Strom Thurmond, R-S.C., a Kennedy opponent, said the shooting "shows the extent to which permissiveness and disregard for law and order have taken our country down the road to anarchy."

Anxious crowds gather at Good Samaritan Hospital to "pray for Bobby" and await word of his condition. Kennedy's press secretary, Frank Mankiewicz, reads somber medical bulletin to newsmen, bottom.

"I'm shocked and horrified by this tragedy," former President Harry S. Truman said in a brief statement released by his personal secretary, Miss Rose Conway. "I fervently hope that he will recover completely."

Governor John Connally of Texas, who was wounded in the barrage that killed John Kennedy, called the shooting of Robert Kennedy "a shocking act of violence" and said:

"In these agonizing hours, Nellie (his wife) and I suffer with Mrs. Ethel Kennedy, their children and the entire Kennedy family."

Patrick Henry, a junior at the State University of New York in Buffalo, voiced a similar cry.

"God! What's going on?" he asked. "It's happening all over again."

Sylvia Coblentz, 26, a Cleveland, Ohio, health educator, told the reporter who informed her of Kennedy's shooting: "I tend to think you're putting me on—I'm sorry." When she was convinced the contender for the Democratic Presidential nomination had been shot, she said:

"I guess the first thing to do is to go someplace and cry."

Mrs. Richard Siegel, leaving an early morning Catholic mass in Tonawanda, N.Y., said: "I had no intention of voting for him, but my heart aches for him and his family."

Evangelist Billy Graham said the shooting of Kennedy was "symbolic of what is happening throughout the country and most of the world."

"I don't weep often," he said at Montreat, N.C., "but today, in this beautiful sunshine, I wept for my country which has declined so much in its morality and spirituality."

Vice President Hubert H. Humphrey, awakened after midnight and told of the shooting, displayed an immediate reaction of horror.

Remaining in his pajamas, he stayed awake most of the remainder of the night, making telephone calls and keeping up on events.

An aide said the first call Humphrey made was to Stephen Smith, a brother-in-law of Kennedy.

The Vice President was in Colorado to deliver the commencement address at the Air Force Academy. He cancelled the appearance early in the morning and—red-eyed and grim-faced—flew back to Washington.

"May God forgive us and help us all," he said in a statement read by Air Force Secretary Harold Brown to the graduating Air Force cadets.

Immediately after learning of the shooting, Humphrey cancelled his appearances for the remainder of the week. Humphrey and Kennedy were opponents in their bid for the Democratic Presidential nomination.

"Our sorrow is for the man and his family, which already has known too much tragedy," Humphrey's statement said. "We can only determine as a free people that such madness shall not recur."

Humphrey called on the nation to pray and to face the full reality of "what this dreadful act means."

"How can we explain these acts within the framework of our free and Democratic society?" he asked.

Humphrey's aides said security restrictions around the Vice President were not increased because of the shooting in Los Angeles, but observers said precautions seemed to be stepped up by Secret Service agents in the entourage.

Humphrey arrived at the airport in a limousine that had taken him from the Air Force Academy, where he had stayed at the visiting officers' quarters. He stepped out of the car almost directly into the plane without a word or a wave to a small crowd watching.

Senator Eugene McCarthy, who with Humphrey opposed Kennedy for the Democratic Presidential nomination, was at his headquarters in the Beverly Hilton hotel at the time of the shooting. He suspended all political activity and said he would return immediately to Washington. He issued a statement saying:

"No words could fully convey the feeling I have toward the Kennedy family at this time of their tragedy. It is not enough to say this is the act of one deranged man if that is the case. The nation I think bears too great a burden of guilt for this kind of violence here in our own land.

"All of us must keep vigil with the nation and pray and hope that Senator Kennedy will recover."

Senator McCarthy arrived at the hospital where Kennedy was being treated about noon in a four-car motorcade led by a police car sounding its siren. He appeared haggard and made no statement there. Pierre Salinger, press secretary for the late President and one of Robert Kennedy's top backers in California, greeted McCarthy in the lobby. The Senator was accompanied by Secret Service men.

Richard M. Nixon, contender for the GOP Presidential nomination, cancelled his appointments for the week and remained in seclusion in his Fifth Avenue apartment under the guard of six Secret Service men in the wake of the assassination attempt against Senator Robert F. Kennedy.

The Secret Service agents were assigned to Nixon on order of President Johnson, who decided all Presidential aspirants should be put under protective guard. They arrived at the Nixon apartment about six hours after Kennedy was gunned down in Los Angeles.

Nixon ordered his national headquarters in New York and his Washington headquarters closed for the day. He cancelled all appointments, including a background briefing with newsmen who have been covering his campaign and a trip to Michigan Friday to attend fund-raising affairs and meet convention delegates.

The former Vice President sent a personal message to Mrs. Robert Kennedy and issued a statement saying: "I am shocked and appalled at the attempt on Senator Kennedy's life. My deepest sympathies go to the Senator's family, which has known more than its share of tragedy. Mrs. Nixon and I join with Americans everywhere in offering our very best wishes for a swift and complete recovery."

World Bank President Robert S. McNamara, who is close to the Robert F. Kennedy family, burst into tears Wednesday at a ceremony marking the signing of a $3 million loan agreement for agricultural development in Costa Rica.

The visiting Costa Rican President, Jose Joaquín Trejos Fernandez, embraced McNamara at the start of the ceremony when the former Defense Secretary started crying, tears streaming down his face. McNamara regained his composure and the ceremony was completed.

Later he said, "I pray God he will recover and that this thing will shock our people to correct those ills which he fought against."

Throughout the nation, there were expressions of deep concern for the country and attempts to pinpoint blame for the shooting.

Mayor Jerome P. Cavanagh of Detroit said the shooting "reveals just how deeply sick America is." Florida Governor Claude Kirk said the nation "is in the throes of anarchy." Mississippi Governor John Bell Williams said "Such deplorable and incredible crimes as this will destroy our country if allowed to continue."

Senator James O. Eastland of Mississippi said the breakdown of law and order "can be traced to decisions by high federal courts which coddle lawbreakers, hamper police and make it almost impossible to convict criminals."

Civil rights leader Charles Evers, whose brother Medgar was assassinated several years ago, blamed racial hatred for the shooting of Kennedy.

Mayor Carl B. Stokes of Cleveland said, "Our prayers are with America that our society will somehow be able to free itself of hate and violence."

Two Communist party leaders, General Secretary Gus Hall and National Chairman Henry Winston, said in a statement: "The pattern of assassinations and attempted assassinations is directed against public figures who in one form or another take a stand against policies of extreme militarism and racism."

Roy Wilkins, executive director of the National Association for the Advancement of Colored People, told Mrs. Kennedy in a message: "Our prayers for Senator Kennedy's full and speedy recovery are inevitably bound up with horror at still another senseless act of violence and with fear lest there be no end of such acts."

Attorney General Frank J. Kelley of Michigan, president of the National Association of Attorneys General, expressed "concern for our country and whether we are going to continue to follow this path of violence or finally at long last accept the rule of law."

Henry Ford II, board chairman of the Ford Motor Co., called the attack on Kennedy "an appalling reflection of the violence that marks our times."

Governor Philip H. Hoff of Vermont said the shooting indicated the nation "must face the harsh realities of hatred and violence in our society." New Jersey Governor Richard J. Hughes urged prayers "that the evil and senseless violence in America will end with this tragedy."

Los Angeles Mayor Sam Yorty said, "This could have happened anywhere." Former Florida Governor LeRoy Collins said, "All Americans stand desecrated when something like this happens."

Mayor Richard J. Daley of Chicago urged Congress to pass a Federal gun law "because there are too many people with guns that should not have them."

Governor Dan K. Moore of North Carolina observed, "It is a tragic turn of events for a democracy when public figures must literally put their lives on the line when they enter the political arena."

In New York, a single word, "SHAME," was shown for two and one-half hours without sound on television sets of home viewers tuning in on WPIX-TV, a local station.

A spokesman for the station, which is owned by the *Daily News*, said that the word was used instead of the usual opening test pattern at 8:30 a.m. because it was felt that the usual children's show of cartoons was inappropriate during the crucial period that Senator Robert Kennedy was in surgery.

At 11 a.m. when news had been received that Kennedy was out of surgery, the station went on the air with news and a documentary.

In Texas, a people deeply touched by the assassination four years and six months ago of President John F. Kennedy were shocked and tearful at news of the shooting and critical wounding of Kennedy's brother Robert in California.

The woman who gave President Lyndon Johnson the oath of office following the death of John Kennedy, U.S. District Judge Sarah Hughes, said, "I think it is shocking. It is terrible. I don't know any of the circumstances. It is unbelievable that it could happen again."

Bill Kilgarlin, prominent Houston liberal Democrat and coordinator of the Harris County campaign for Robert Kennedy, said in Houston, "Of course, your initial reaction is one of disbelief. It just cannot happen twice in the same family. I think my second reaction is one of shock about how insane this all is. How a civilized people—supposedly a civilized people—how we resort to violence. We are supposedly one of the bulwarks of democracy in the world. How useless, how unnecessary it is to nip off in the prime of life somebody such as this."

The Rev. William Stack, a Roman Catholic priest in Dallas, said, "I will hold a mass for him (Kennedy) today. I am shocked beyond words that such a terrible thing would happen."

"The world is mad," said Ed Bakewell, a flight information man at Love Field Airport in Dallas. "It is a shame that we have to resort to expressing our opinion of people by bullets instead of ballots."

A nurse in Parkland Hospital emergency room, to which John Kennedy was taken Nov. 22, 1963, Mrs. Mary East, said, "I think it was a terrible thing (the Robert Kennedy shooting), and I feel bad about it."

Dr. Earl Rose, a medical examiner at the time of John Kennedy's death in Dallas, said, "Oh, my God. That is tragic . . . terrible. This is terrible and unspeakable."

Dr. Malcolm Perry, who helped treat John Kennedy in Dallas, said the shooting of Kennedy's brother was "terrible."

In Alabama, third-party Presidential candidate George Wallace called the shooting "another tragic blot on American history."

The former Alabama Governor said, "It is symptomatic of the lawlessness and violence which has invaded our nation and threatens to destroy

The newspaper headlines read:

THE DALLAS TIMES HERALD — FINAL EDITION

Gunman Seized

NEDY SHOT DOWN

Slug Lodges Assassin Won't Talk, Give Name
Inside Brain

At the spot in Dallas where President John F. Kennedy was assassinated, a vacationer reads the new tragic headlines.

the political system nourished by the freedoms enjoyed by Americans. It must be stopped.

"My sincere prayer is for the recovery of Senator Kennedy and the others wounded in this tragic event."

In Boston, Richard Cardinal Cushing, Archbishop of Boston and personal friend of the Kennedys who said mass at the late President's funeral, dedicated a day of prayer that the New York Senator's life might be saved.

"I pray that it will never happen again," he said. Then he added, "We did that before, too."

In Washington, shocked and angry poverty campaigners organized a march on the headquarters of the National Rifle Association to denounce it for lobbying against gun-control legislation.

The attack on Kennedy, coming two months after the assassination of Dr. Martin Luther King Jr., outraged residents of Resurrection City, campsite of the Poor People's Campaign.

Their leaders announced that the march was getting underway at 11:30 a.m. but later changed their plans and decided to eat lunch at the camp before setting out for the rifle association's headquarters in a modernistic new office building on 16th Street in Northwest Washington.

The Reverend Ralph David Abernathy, "Mayor" of the shantytown, conducted a prayer service for Kennedy's recovery. He said the shooting was "a terrible tragedy" for the poor of America.

"He was one of the precious few leaders of national stature who have been trying to do something effective to end poverty and oppression in our society."

At the United Nations, the Security Council Wednesday night adjourned an urgent meeting on the latest Middle East flareup in respect to Senator Kennedy, who was shot by a man identified as a Jordanian.

The assassination attempt occurred on the first anniversary of the June 5-11 Arab-Israeli War of 1967.

Before postponing discussion of border fighting between Israel and Jordan that erupted Tuesday, the council expressed its "sense of shock and deep sorrow" at the attempted assassination of the brother of the late President.

American Ambassador Arthur J. Goldberg, the Council president for June, read a telegram he sent to Mrs. Ethel Kennedy on behalf of the 15-nation body.

It conveyed the "sense of shock and deep sorrow which all members feel at the grievous news of the attempt to assassinate your husband.

"Senator Kennedy's support for the United Nations and its purposes of peace is known and respected throughout the world. All members of the Council join me in hoping and praying for him and in profound sympathy for you and for the entire Kennedy family."

UN Secretary General U Thant said it was incomprehensible to him that violence should continually jeopardize "the lives of the finest men" in the United States.

Thant made the statement in a telegram to Mrs. Robert F. Kennedy in which he said he had learned with horror and dismay of the shooting of the Senator and would pray for his recovery.

Thant and General Assembly President Corneliu Manescu of Romania sent separate messages of sympathy to Mrs. Kennedy.

Dr. Ralph Bunche, UN Undersecretary, told newsmen it was "intolerable" that in a great society such as the United States there should be violence of this kind.

Diplomats in the corridors discussed the attempt on Kennedy's life and expressed puzzlement at what one of them termed the "increasing frequency" of assassinations in the United States.

At Vatican City, Pope Paul VI deplored Wednesday the attempt on the life of Senator Kennedy. He said he was praying "for the life and health of this young man who was offering himself to the public service in his country."

The Pontiff spoke to a vast crowd gathered for his weekly general audience in St. Peter's Basilica. There were hundreds of Americans in the crowd. Many of them knew nothing of the Los Angeles shooting and gasped aloud when the Pope made his statement in English.

"We deplore this new manifestation of violence and terror," the Pope declared.

Then he spoke in Italian, expressing similar sentiments and praying that "the means of violence and crime will be banished from the world."

Vatican sources said the Pope was "shocked and deeply saddened."

Earlier the Pontiff had asked James Francis Cardinal McIntyre, Archbishop of Los Angeles, "to present to the federal authorities and the beloved Kennedy family sentiments of paternal concern." He also asked the Cardinal to keep him informed on Kennedy's condition.

The Vatican newspaper *L'Osservatore Romano* said Kennedy was a symbol and "striking him down doesn't destroy the reality that is maturing".

"The new act of violence which stains the American political scene with blood arouses feelings of pity, deploration, and horror in all free men, in whoever recognized the value of life and freedom," the paper said in an editorial.

At Amman, Jordan, Palestinians voiced fear that a "wave of anti-Arab hysteria" in the United States and other Western nations might follow allegations that a Jordanian Arab shot Senator Kennedy.

"Jewish propaganda" was one Palestinian Arab's first reaction to news that Sirhan Bishara Sirhan, 24, had been arraigned on an attempted murder charge.

"It's outrageous," declared Mahmoud El-Sharif, editor of Amman's semi-official newspaper *Ad-Destour*. "What Arab in his right mind would do a thing like this. The only people to benefit from such actions are the Jews."

Some Palestinians expressed the belief that Sirhan was a "hired killer" and part of a Zionist plot to discredit the Arabs.

One young Palestinian said: "Let him (Kennedy) die. Our people are living in tents because the Americans gave jets to the Jews."

Reports said Sirhan's family came from the area adjacent to Jerusalem's Wailing Wall, where Israelis bulldozed hundreds of Arab houses to make room for visiting tourists following the Mideast war of 1967.

Around the world men wept for the fallen Senator and lamented for the future of the United States.

In London, Sammy Davis Jr. told a theater audience Wednesday night after act one that his show *Golden Boy* could not go on with him because his heart "for once was not in the theater (but) many miles away in America." Weeping, he walked offstage.

In Santiago, President Eduardo Frei of Chile said every man felt the blow that struck Kennedy. "I believe this has caused all the men in the world to tremble."

In Great Britain, where even the police do not carry guns, a shocked London bobby reads of the latest violence in the United States.

The grief, the groping for words of condolence, the sadness came easier to a shocked world than did understanding.

"Why? Why? Why?" said *The Daily Mirror* of London. "What is this dreadful sickness that lurks beneath the surface of the richest country on earth?"

In Cape Town, South Africa, Mrs. Helen Suzman, the only member of Parliament who votes against apartheid racial policies, said, "It is a further example of the ghastly undercurrent of violence that seems to be one of the hazards of public office in America and elsewhere. Robert Kennedy's fearlessness would make him more vulnerable than most."

In Amsterdam, Foreign Minister Joseph Luns of Holland said, "One wonders whether in the United States a society of violence is growing."

In Buenos Aires, former President Arturo Frondizi of Argentina said, "This brutal attempt reveals the desperation of warlike and racist elements, agents of international monopolies."

But mostly the voices from around the world expressed puzzlement.

In Helsinki, Prime Minister Mauno Koivisto of Finland said the world is "worried and frightened at the alarming increase of violence in the United States." In Oslo, Prime Minister Per Borten of Norway said, "The question obviously arises what can be the reason behind such bursts of violence even in countries built on democracy and with guarantees for justice and security for the individual citizens."

In Rangoon, Foreign Minister U Thi Han of Burma said, "There is too much shooting in America."

In Tokyo, Professor Hiroshi Nakatani, who knew Kennedy, said, "The image of democratic state that the Japanese people have had in America is crumbled."

In Hong Kong, the newspaper *The Standard* said: "The vast majority of Americans are honest, fine people. The weakness of America is that too many of these upright people are too rigid in their ideas and outlooks. This can lead to passion, hatred—and disaster. Perhaps a touch of oriental nonchalance might be good for America."

In West Germany, Foreign Minister Willy Brandt said the Kennedy family had been smitten "as if in a Greek tragedy."

Moscow radio blamed it on "the notorious freedom of the capitalist society—the freedom to kill." Russian citizens asked Americans at the Moscow Trade Fair, "What is happening in the United States? What kind of country have you?"

Women wept on a street in Rio de Janeiro.

Many linked the shooting of Kennedy to the assassinations of President John F. Kennedy and Dr. Martin Luther King Jr.

Prime Minister Hilmar Baunsgaard of Denmark asked, "What kind of world do we live in? This is symptomatic of an increase in violence."

A student at Stockholm University, Ulf Johansson, said, "After Kennedy and King, this was the logical continuation."

A Tokyo sales clerk, Mrs. Yukiko Kumagai, cried, "No, not again!"

From Moscow to Oslo, people on the street said the gun was still the law in America "like the Wild West."

The East German news agency said "In the 'freest' nation in the world murder has become a political tool."

"I never knew American politics was so much involved in violence," said Deputy Prime Minister Tun Abdul Razak of Malaysia.

"Will this murdering craze never stop?" asked the Paris newspaper *Le Monde.* "With the exception of Lincoln Rockwell (American Nazi leader), the victims of violence all have been liberal thinkers . . . men who reflect the image we like to have of the U.S. abroad."

Tokyo newspapers rushed out with extras and straphanging subway riders read the news. Tokyo television viewers saw the bleeding Kennedy's face beamed across the Pacific via satellite.

Radio and television stations interrupted programs to give minute-by-minute bulletins on Kennedy's condition in Vienna, Brussels, Warsaw, Dublin, Stockholm, Prague, Budapest and Belgrade.

Norwegians crowded around newsstands in Oslo, one man saying, "This tendency to use force may endanger a whole society."

The president of the Italian Parliament called the UPI Bureau in Rome to confirm the news and then announced it to a shocked Assembly.

Crowds gathered on the streets of Dublin murmuring, "I just can't believe it."

Construction workers in Helsinki laid down their tools to listen to the news on car radios. People in Budapest streets crowded around radios in cars parked in the middle of the streets.

GIs on leave from Vietnam huddled around radios in the USO lounge in Tokyo. Newspapers in Johannesburg, South Africa, were swamped with telephone calls.

A member of the Dunlanstown, Ireland, city council took the news to the Kennedy cousins. The family knelt in prayer.

Messages of sympathy sped to the Kennedy family from West German President Heinrich Luebke, British Prime Minister Harold Wilson, Premier Indira Gandhi of India, King Hassan II of Morocco, President Eamon De Valera of Ireland, President Tito of Yugoslavia and Premier George Papadopoulos of Greece.

Expressions of "dreadful shock" came from Turkish Premier Suleyman Demirel, Dutch Premier Piet de Jong and Deputy Prime Minister John McEwen of Australia.

Violence in America

Psychologists, sociologists, educators, histo-rians, clergymen, and political leaders agree that Americans "love to fight."

by Ronald G. Cohen

"We are a violent people with a violent history, and the instinct for violence has seeped into the bloodstream of our national life," said Arthur Schlesinger Jr., the Pulitzer Prize-winning historian who was an aide to the late President John F. Kennedy.

"The whole culture has changed the violence syndrome into a cool, guiltless routine of disposing of problems by disposing of the people who cause the problems," said Albert Bandura, a psychologist and professor at Stanford University.

"I don't weep often, but today, in this beautiful sunshine, I wept for my country that has declined so much in its morality and spirituality," said evangelist Billy Graham.

"What in the nature of our people and the environment of our society makes possible such murder and violence?" asked President Johnson in announcing the appointment of a high-level commission to study violence in America—"this tragic phenomenon."

These men all spoke in the flush of disbelief that swept the nation after the shooting of Senator Robert F. Kennedy. They spoke in sorrow, but they spoke with reason and restraint.

They expressed the increasingly widespread belief that violence is not an occasional isolated tragedy, but is ingrained—perhaps irreversibly—in the fabric of American life.

Black Power advocate H. Rap Brown said it several months ago:

"Violence is as American as cherry pie."

Psychologists, sociologists, educators, historians, clergymen, replying to a UPI survey, seemed to agree.

"You talk about the good old pioneer days . . . but we don't live in the old pioneer days when everybody's a vigilante and you shoot them up," said Senator Joseph Tydings, D-Md.

"I think we've got to come to our senses."

Others agreed that the preoccupation with guns and violence might be almost an American phenomenon.

Dr. David Abrahamsen, a governor of the Lemberg Center for the Study of Violence at Brandeis University, said Americans not only condone violence, "We love it."

"We love to fight. The frontier days made the gun manly," he said. "In France they can riot for three weeks and only two people get killed. Can you imagine how many would have been killed here?"

Abrahamson said America's stress on materialism breeds violence.

"We're not a melting pot, we're a damned pressure cooker. Our society is not built on the restraints of family or class, it's built on success. If you don't have it, you're frustrated.

"Frustration. The wet nurse of violence."

Several authorities said that television and other mass media must share the blame for the violence syndrome in the nation.

Stanford's Bandura, an expert on the impact of television violence on children, called it "a Frankenstein monster."

"I don't understand how we can stop it," he said. "I remember testimony (at Senate hearings) in which a mother was explaining to her daughter, brought up on television, that her grandfather had died. She testified that the little girl's reaction was 'Who shot him?' "

Dr. Herbert A. Otto, a Chicago psychologist, said the continued stress on violence by mass media is making "America accept violent acts as commonplace."

A recent study of 195 television cartoons, he said, showed 1,430 acts of violence, including killings, physical assaults, verbal assaults and harmful pranks.

"The most impressionable members of the nation, the youth of America, can often be found viewing cartoons where violence is being perpetrated at about the rate of one violent incident every 50 seconds," Otto said.

A psychiatrist from Chicago, Dr. Thaddens Kostruba, agreed: "Every TV Western has a murder."

Dr. Kenneth Keniston, a Yale Medical Center psychologist, said the television set has given to violence an "immediacy" that "secretly interests and pleases" many persons.

Dr. Carlton W. Orchinik, mental health consultant for the Philadelphia County Court, said he believes that television does not encourage violence but brings about an indifference to it.

"We can see scene after scene of gangsterism, and we can ignore it because it does not seem to touch us."

Schlesinger, a close friend of Robert Kennedy, spoke Wednesday at commencement exercises for 48 doctoral graduates at the City University of New York.

He called the American people "the most frightening on this planet."

"We are a frightening people because we have already in this decade murdered the two of our citizens (President Kennedy and Dr. Martin Luther King Jr.) who stood pre-eminently before the world as the embodiments of American idealism—and because last night we tried to murder a third."

"We are a frightening people because the atrocities we commit trouble so little our official self-righteousness, our invincible conviction of our moral infallibility," Schlesinger said.

"It is almost as if a primal curse has been fixed on our nation. We are a violent people with a violent history, and the instinct for violence has seeped into the bloodstream of our national life."

Dr. Arnold Freedman, chief of psychological services at the Veterans Administration Hospital in Pittsburgh, called violence "a reflection of our emphasis on competition as a way of life as opposed to cooperation—like two dogs who fight over a scrap of bread rather than share what they have."

"With the competitive urge you are bound to get aggression and hostility," he added. "Competition is useful since it encourages us to produce. But this is a cost of tearing people down."

A sociology professor from the University of Vermont, Dr. Jeremy Felt, said the shooting of Robert Kennedy was "entirely consistent with the violent history of America," adding that violence has been practically "institutionalized" in the nation through America's cowboy-and-Indian folklore.

A University of Vermont colleague, Dr. M. W. Perrine, a professor of psychology, agreed.

He traced the violent settling of grievances back to the days of the early West. So did Dr. Michael O. Sawyer, professor of criminal law at Syracuse University.

Dr. John Spiegel, director of Brandeis University's Lemberg Center, blamed the assassination attempt on the nation's "gun fetish."

He said there is an emotional addiction to use guns, "as strong as any other addiction, such as drugs." He said there was also an "emotional habituation to use violence in general, particularly through gunfire, in the resolution of conflicts."

His colleague at the center, Dr. Ralph W. Conant, said that since the assassination of Lincoln in 1865, one-fifth of America's presidents have been murdered and one-third have had attempts made on their lives.

Louis W. Koenig, professor of government at New York University, said assassinations tend to be attempted by persons "who have their own slant on public policy, then take it out on public officials or candidates for office."

Some felt blaming an entire nation was too broad an indictment for the atrocity of a single person.

California Governor Ronald Reagan said he was in "great disagreement" with those who believe Americans would feel "a collective sense of guilt" for Kennedy's assassination. On a national television program Wednesday night he deplored the shooting as "senseless and savage," but added:

"Two-hundred million Americans did not do this. One young man did it, and for not even an American reason," a reference to the fact the alleged gunman was an anti-Israeli Jordanian exile from Jerusalem.

Dr. Fernando G. Torgerson, director of the School of Social Work at the University of Texas at Arlington, said he did not believe assassinations are part of the nature of America.

"These are guys who are completely crazy. America is not at all a violent society."

Even President Johnson, in his national address, absolved Americans of a collective blame in the rash of assassinations and assassination attempts.

But he said it would be "wrong—it would be self-deceptive—to ignore the connection between lawlessness, hatred and this act of violence."

DEATH

Thursday, June 6, 1968

Weeping for a fallen leader.

The Final Moments

Kennedy fails to rally from
three-hour brain operation.

by Paul R. Jeschke

LOS ANGELES (UPI) . . . Robert F. Kennedy died today of an assassin's bullet.

Death came for the boyish-faced Senator at 1:44 a.m., an agonizingly long 25 hours and 29 minutes after he had been wounded. He failed to rally from a three-hour operation that had sought to remove from his brain fragments of the .22-caliber death bullet.

The 42-year-old Kennedy died in a starkly bare cubicle in the fifth floor intensive care ward of Good Samaritan Hospital, an Episcopalian institution. Curtains had been drawn around the glass and metal walls of the cubicle to give some privacy in the tiny room, whose main furnishing was the collapsible-sided hospital bed on which he lay. A metal wall lamp over the bed provided light. At the end the Rev. Thomas Pecha of Los Angeles administered Extreme Unction of the Roman Catholic Church.

Members of the Kennedy family gathered about his bed. They included: his wife Ethel, expecting their eleventh child in seven months; his only surviving brother, Ted—Senator Edward M. Kennedy of Massachusetts; his widowed sister-in-law Jacqueline, who less than five years earlier had cradled in her lap the bloody head of President John Kennedy as he died from a grimly similar assassination; his sisters, Mrs. Stephen Smith and Mrs. Patricia Lawford; and his brother-in-law, Stephen Smith, who had helped manage his political campaigns. Ethel was reported by a priest to be "bearing up very well," but an obstetrician stood by in case he was needed.

81

Other members of the family, including the three oldest Kennedy children, and close friends had maintained a vigil nearby in the hospital's paneled board-of-directors room. They had waited, sprawling in the deeply cushioned gold chairs or pacing the gold carpeting, as they prayed for a miracle that did not happen.

Outside the hospital a crowd of Kennedy's admirers silently moved about carrying "Pray for Bobby" signs.

At 2 a.m. Frank Mankiewicz, the Senator's press aide, entered an auditorium across the street from the hospital to speak to reporters awaiting bulletins on Kennedy's condition.

"I have a short announcement to read, which I will read at this time," said the haggard Mankiewicz. "Senator Robert Francis Kennedy died at 1:44 a.m. today, June 6, 1968. He was 42 years old."

The hushed reception to these words was in sharp contrast to the wild enthusiasm of the crowds who had been attracted by the Senator in his campaign for the Presidency with a call of "I come to ask your help— these are not ordinary times."

THE WHITE HOUSE
Death of Robert F. Kennedy
By the President of the United States of America

𝔄 𝔓roclamation

To the People of the United States:

A noble and compassionate leader, a good and faithful servant of the people, in the full vigor of his promise, lies dead from an assassin's bullet.

The tragedy and the senseless violence of Robert F. Kennedy's death casts a deep shadow of grief across America and across the world.

This is a moment for all Americans to join hands and walk together through this dark night of common anguish into a new dawn of healing unity.

NOW, THEREFORE, I, Lyndon B. Johnson, President of the United States, do call upon all Americans to observe Sunday next, the ninth day of June, as a day of national mourning in his memory throughout the United States. In our churches, in our homes, and in our hearts let us resolve before God and before each other that the purpose of progress and justice for which Robert F. Kennedy lived shall endure.

I DIRECT THAT until interment the flag of the United States shall be flown at half-staff on all buildings, grounds and naval vessels of the Federal Government in the District of Columbia and throughout the United States and its territories and possessions.

I ALSO DIRECT that the flag shall be flown at half-staff for the same length of time at all United States embassies, legations, consular offices, and other facilities abroad, including all military facilities and naval vessels and stations.

IN WITNESS WHEREOF, I have hereunto set my hand this sixth day of June, in the year of Our Lord Nineteen Hundred and Sixty-eight and of the independence of the United States of America the one hundred and ninety-second.

LYNDON B. JOHNSON.
THE WHITE HOUSE.

Autopsy Report

*Had he lived, Kennedy
would have been crippled.*

LOS ANGELES (UPI) . . . The bullet wound in the brain of Senator Robert F. Kennedy was so severe that even if he had lived there would have been "extensive damage," Los Angeles County Medical Examiner Thomas Noguchi said Thursday.

"Scattered fragments of the bullet and bone tissue damaged the main portion of the right side of the brain," said the coroner. He refused to comment specifically on whether there might have been impairment of eyesight, speech and movement, but said "the injury was so severe as to cause extensive damage."

Noguchi said all the vital organs were removed from Kennedy's body, including the entire brain, and retained here for further pathological examination.

The complete autopsy report will not be finished for a few weeks, said Noguchi. "It must be thorough. Let me emphasize that we have the very best of facilities," he said.

Noguchi, two pathologists on his staff, and three medical consultants from the Armed Forces Institute of Pathology in Washington, D.C., started the autopsy at 3 a.m. and completed it at 9:15 a.m.

"Hundreds and hundreds of colored pictures were taken," said Noguchi.

The formal autopsy bulletin said:

"The cause of death is ascribed by me as a gunshot wound of the right mastoid penetrating the brain. Complete findings will be contained in the official autopsy report."

Noguchi said it was undetermined which bullet struck Kennedy first.

One small caliber bullet entered the back portion of the right arm pit and traveled upward. It lodged just beneath the flesh of Kennedy's neck. That bullet was removed and turned over to the police. It tore through layers of muscle tissue but did not penetrate any vital organs.

The other bullet entered the brain.

Surgeons worked three hours to remove the fragments of metal and shattered bone. A small fragment of the bullet remained in the mid-skull area. Noguchi refused to describe the trajectory of the fatal wound. He said that further microscopic tests would be conducted on the vital organs and brain tissue.

Procedures for the autopsy were discussed in a meeting attended by the county coroner, the district attorney, and various representatives of the Kennedy family.

Purpose of the discussions was to forestall the questions raised in the aftermath of the assassination of President John F. Kennedy by fully disclosing the results and conducting a thorough autopsy.

Noguchi said the brain surgery by the team of six neurosurgeons trying to save the Senator's life was "amazing and very delicate." He said that the artery that supplies the cerebellum was severed and that there was no doubt other arteries in the brain were involved.

Astronaut John Glenn entertains younger Kennedy children while funeral party with older children boards plane in Los Angeles.

Going Home

Presidential jet carries Kennedy's body
and mourners on transcontinental flight.

by Jack V. Fox

LOS ANGELES (UPI) . . . Mourning family and friends accompanied the body of Robert F. Kennedy home today to the state of New York, which he had represented as Senator.

The African mahogany casket bearing Kennedy's body was placed aboard an Air Force 707 jet that had been sent by President Johnson. The four-engine airliner took off from Los Angeles International Airport at 1:28 p.m. As the plane taxied down the runway many persons in the crowd at the airport were crying. A white youth put his arm around a sobbing Negro woman attempting to comfort her.

The plane earlier had been scheduled to depart at 10 a.m., but was delayed by the lengthy autopsy acquiesced to by his widow to avoid any controversy such as the one still surrounding the slaying of President Kennedy in Dallas.

During the wait for the completion of the autopsy and embalming, Senator Edward Kennedy—the only one of the brothers still left to carry the political banner—picked out a mahogany casket. It was covered with maroon draping.

A cortege of a blue hearse and nine limousines with police motorcycle escorts left Good Samaritan Hospital at 12:40 p.m. for the 20-mile freeway trip to the airport. Ethel and Jacqueline Kennedy rode in the front limousine.

Several hundred persons had gathered outside the hospital for a farewell to the Senator who was struck down in his moment of political victory in the California Presidential primary. Many threw flowers into the path of the hearse, but most members of the crowd were grimly quiet in contrast to the exuberance they exhibited during his campaign when they tore at his clothes, mussed his hair, and pulled off his shoes in their enthusiasm.

Secret Service agents and white-helmeted Los Angeles policemen were stationed at strategic locations near the hospital and at the airport, where thousands gathered for the departure of the plane.

A red carpet leading to the sleek Air Force jet was lined with roses and carnations. The flowers had been placed there by an unidentified woman shortly before the cortege arrived at the airport. Members of the Kennedy family accompanied the casket aboard the rear of the plane on a lift vehicle. Others making the flight to New York went up a portable stairway at the front.

For Pierre Salinger, former press secretary of President Kennedy, the flight aboard this Presidential plane was especially poignant because it was the same craft that had been carrying him and members of the Cabinet to Japan when word was received of the President's assassination in 1963, and it had had to turn around in flight over the Pacific and carry the party back to Washington for John Kennedy's funeral.

A group of 71 friends and staff were invited to travel on today's funeral flight. Their names read like a cross-section of *Who's Who* in the fields of government, politics, the arts, show business, and sports. Other than members of the plane's crew, those on the flight were:

Mrs. Robert F. Kennedy, and her three oldest children, Kathleen, Joseph, and Robert.

Mrs. John F. Kennedy.

Senator Edward M. Kennedy.

Mr. and Mrs. Stephen Smith, Mr. Kennedy's sister and brother-in-law.

Prince and Princess Stanislas Radziwill, Mrs. John F. Kennedy's sister and her husband.

Mr. and Mrs. James Whittaker. He was the first American to climb Mount Everest.

Mr. and Mrs. Edwin O. Guthman, national editor of The Los Angeles *Times* and his wife.

John Siegenthaler, editor of the Nashville *Tennesseean*.

Burke Marshall, former deputy attorney general.

Frank Mankiewicz, Mr. Kennedy's press secretary.

Rafer Johnson, former Olympic star.

Roosevelt Grier, Los Angeles Rams tackle.

K. LeMoyne Billings, New York advertising executive.

Richard N. Goodwin, a speechwriter for both slain Kennedys.

Mrs. Pat Lawford, sister of Mr. Kennedy.

Fernando Para, a Mexican architect.

Charles Evers, NAACP official, of Mississippi.

Mr. and Mrs. Jesse M. Unruh, the Speaker of the California Assembly and his wife.

Mr. and Mrs. Andy Williams, the singer and his wife.

Mr. and Mrs. George Plimpton, the author and his wife.

Charles Spaulding, New York investment banker.

Mrs. Martin Luther King Jr.

Mr. and Mrs. Pierre Salinger.

John Douglas, son of former Senator Paul Douglas.

Ethel Kennedy slept by her husband's coffin on flight, according to TV newsman.

NEW YORK (UPI) . . . Mrs. Robert F. Kennedy, during the flight bringing her husband's body to New York, chatted with other passengers and later fell asleep beside her husband's coffin, according to a newsman aboard the plane.

Sander Vanocur, an NBC television newsman and friend of the Kennedy family, said on a network broadcast Thursday night that during the flight Mrs. Kennedy spent about half an hour talking with her sister-in-law, Jacqueline Kennedy.

"And then after that was over, Mrs. Robert F. Kennedy walked down the aisle, stopping with various people along the way, in the aft section of the cabin, just talking to them, sitting with them—I use the word 'joking' with them, because that's what she did," Vanocur said.

"She was in remarkably good spirits. I suspect she's been under sedation for the last . . . I guess 24 or 25 hours."

"I suppose everybody was trying to keep her mind off what happened," Vanocur said.

Vanocur described Senator Edward Kennedy as angry over his brother's assassination.

"I think he was mostly—he's mad. I might as well say it, he's mad," Vanocur said. "He's mad at what happens in this country. He does not know whether it is the act of a single person, or whether this is the act of a conspiracy."

Vanocur's description of the flight was the only one to come from a newsman aboard the plane. The late Senator Robert Kennedy's press secretary, Frank Mankiewicz, later indicated the Kennedys were disturbed by his reporting of events during the flight.

"Everyone on the plane was there on the basis of friendship," Mankiewicz said in response to questions about Vanocur's description of the flight from Los Angeles.

"There were only friends, colleagues and staff members. Nobody was there as a reporter," he said. "The plane was private and that is how we view it. We are not going to comment on anything said on the airplane."

In his television broadcast Vanocur said Mrs. John F. Kennedy "thought for a moment it was the same plane" on which she flew to Washington with her own husband's body after his assassination in Dallas in 1963. It was pointed out that the Presidential jet, one of several, actually was the one in which Secretary of State Dean Rusk was flying to Tokyo when he received word that President John F. Kennedy had been shot.

Vanocur said Senator Edward Kennedy remained beside his dead brother's coffin in the plane's forward cabin throughout the flight "and other people took their turns in just lying next to the coffin . . ."

He said about an hour before the plane arrived in New York Edward Kennedy fell asleep "and Mrs. Robert F. Kennedy came up and lay against the coffin." When a Kennedy friend, mountaineer Jim Whittaker, put a pillow under her head, "she woke up for a moment, looked at him, then fell asleep against the coffin," Vanocur said.

Return to New York

*Admirers line silent streets
to welcome Kennedy home.*

by George J. Marder

NEW YORK (UPI) . . . Thousands of grieving New Yorkers watched in silence and often in tears the arrival Thursday night of the body of assassinated Robert F. Kennedy.

The silver and blue Presidential jet carrying the funeral party landed at La Guardia Airport at 8:58 p.m., after a four-and-a-half-hour flight from Los Angeles.

More than a thousand persons waited at the airport in muggy 83-degree heat, including Governor Nelson Rockefeller, Senator Jacob Javits, Mayor John Lindsay, UN Ambassador Arthur Goldberg, and former Secretary of Defense Robert S. McNamara. But the welcome was kept simple at the request of the Kennedy family.

After the jet rolled to a halt, Senator Edward Kennedy was the first to appear in the front door of the plane with two of his slain brother's children, 15-year-old Joseph P. III, and 14-year-old Robert Jr. The three helped move the coffin onto a lift which lowered it and them to a truck. In the effort of transferring the coffin to a platform beside the waiting hearse, one of the Kennedy boys lost his balance. Several persons grabbed him as he began to fall. The crowd gasped.

Other Kennedys descended from the plane by ramp. Ethel Kennedy appeared strained but composed. Mrs. John F. Kennedy was one of the last to leave the plane, remaining in the background. They were joined by Kennedys who had been unable to fly to Los Angeles, including Mrs. Edward Kennedy, as well as the Senator's sister, Mrs. Eunice Shriver, and her husband, U.S. Ambassador to France Sargent Shriver, who had arrived from Paris a short time before. The general expressions of the Kennedy party were vacant and staring. There were no tears.

Before the coffin was loaded into a gray Cadillac hearse, Roman Catholic Archbishop Terence J. Cooke intoned a brief prayer. Family and intimates stood by with bowed heads. Television lights gave the night scene an unnatural brilliance. The coffin was covered with a rich maroon cloth on which was placed a simple bouquet of small white lilies, carnations, and daisies provided by Mrs. Paul Mellon, wife of the banker-philanthropist.

New York police, 250 strong, imposed extreme security on the airport area. For a while they refused to let out-of-town newsmen who had covered Kennedy's campaign and preceded the Presidential jet to New York enter the press area. There were nearly as many newsmen of all media on hand as police and spectators.

Among the spectators was Mrs. Frances Williams, a Negro of Deer Park, N.Y., with boy and girl twins aged 2½. She said she knew her children would not understand what they were seeing now. "But I will be able to tell them he was a very great man," she said. "I hope he did not die in vain and that we learn to make a better world."

Former Olympic champion Rafer Johnson and other friends assisted in placing the casket in the hearse. Senator Edward Kennedy slid into the front seat next to the driver and helped in Ethel Kennedy to sit beside him.

Then the cortege of 34 cars moved out of the airport and headed toward Manhattan, where Kennedy had established a home less than four years ago when he ran for Senator. The caravan was led by a police motorcycle escort and a squad car with a flashing red light.

Tens of thousands of persons lined the 9-mile route, standing under street lamps, often in small family groups. Hundreds stood along the walkways of the Triborough Bridge over which the cortege traveled at about 30 miles an hour. As the hearse passed through a corner of Spanish Harlem on its way to East River Drive, hundreds of Puerto Ricans shouted "Viva!" for their fallen friend.

The entire block around St. Patrick's Cathedral had been closed off to the public by police. When the cortege reached the cathedral, the Kennedy men and boys, joined by a few close friends, carried the casket up the steps in the semi-darkness amid the popping flashes of photographers' flash bulbs. Newsmen and television crews were kept outside the bronze doors of the cathedral.

The Senator's 77-year-old mother, Mrs. Joseph P. Kennedy, who had arrived in New York earlier in the day from Hyannis Port, Mass., joined

Carrying the casket from the plane at La Guardia Airport in New York.

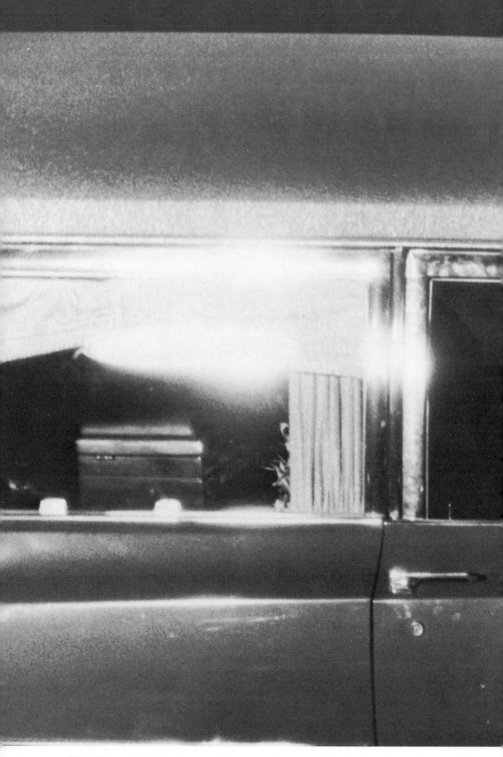

Ethel Kennedy in front seat of hearse on its way from La Guardia to St. Patrick's Cathedral.

Kennedy's two oldest sons and his brother, Edward, help carry the casket into St. Patrick's Cathedral.

Archbishop Terence Cooke (wearing miter) blesses casket as it is carried into the Cathedral.

The slain senator's surviving brother, widow, and oldest son leave St. Patrick's after private services.

14-year-old Robert Jr. helps his 77-year-old-grandmother down the steps of the Cathedral.

her family for a private service at the side of the casket. She wore a black veil over her face and leaned heavily on the arm of her grandson, Joseph P. III. Mrs. Martin Luther King Jr. was with the family.

After the service, the Kennedys went by motorcade to the Waldorf-Astoria Hotel, passing a number of store windows displaying portraits of the slain Senator draped in black crepe.

Thousands of New Yorkers in shirt sleeves and summer dresses remained standing all night behind police barricades on the sidewalks around St. Patrick's, waiting for the cathedral to be opened in the morning for public homage to the Senator. When police told one Negro woman to stay behind the barrier, she said, "Don't push me, that's no way to be now."

The Surviving Brother

Now it falls to Ted to pick up the torch so tragically knocked from the hands of his three elder brothers. Will he become President?

Ted is the only one left.

Of Ambassador Joseph P. Kennedy's four sons, for whom he had unlimited hopes, only the youngest survives—Senator Edward M. Kennedy of Massachusetts.

Two have been slain by assassins and the third died a hero in World War II.

"Let the torch pass to Ted," the Henryetta Daily *Free Lance* said today in a page-one editorial written by publisher J. Leland Gourley, an Oklahoma gubernatorial candidate in 1966.

"This is not just an emotional canonization of the Kennedy name in a moment of shock, shame and the almost hopelessly blemished conscience of this republic," the editorial stated.

". . . We must move with dispatch to convert sorrow to resolution, shift from shock to national uplift, pull ourselves from the muck and mire of disgrace onto the high road of reasoned principle . . .

"The Kennedys, not the name but the men, offered of all things hope: hope for the downtrodden and depressed of the world.

". . . We are not endorsing Ted Kennedy for President as a means of this nation paying a debt to the Kennedys but to paraphrase one of the Kennedys: 'It is not what this nation can do for Ted Kennedy but what Ted Kennedy can do for this nation.'"

Two Democrats who had disagreed on the choice of a Presidential candidate suggested Thursday Edward Kennedy for Vice-President on a ticket headed by Hubert H. Humphrey.

The possibility was raised separately by Representative Clarence Long, D-Md., an early backer of Vice President Humphrey for the nomination, and by Armistead Boothe, who was Virginia manager for Robert F. Kennedy's Presidential Campaign.

Long's office said he had sent Humphrey a telegram urging the selection of the Massachusetts Senator.

Boothe said in Richmond, Va., "It's possible that if the Kennedy name did appear on the ballot, we would have a uniting of the country that we would not have in any other way."

Long also stressed unity in his message to Humphrey and said selection of Kennedy would be a tribute to a family "which has lost three sons in the service of our country."

Being a Kennedy, and the son of a man who expects nothing less, Ted is sure to try to carry on the Kennedy tradition.

Ted, who hates to be called "Teddy," turned 36 on George Washington's last birthday. He is a respected and liked member of the U.S. Senate.

He was elected to the Senate in 1962 to fill the same seat his brother had given up for the Presidency. In 1964, despite a close brush with death in a plane crash, he won reelection for a full term by an overwhelming margin.

In the Senate, he has behaved as the establishment thinks a freshman Senator should—quietly and diffidently. Because of this and his diligent work, he is more popular than Senator Robert F. Kennedy ever was on Capitol Hill.

Regarded as a team player (Bobby was a loner) Ted heads judiciary subcommittees on the aging and on refugees. He has made the problems of the refugees of the war in Vietnam his major concern.

Although affable, smiling and easy-mannered in the Senate—more so than either of his brothers—Ted has avoided the limelight. At the beginning he was very conscious of being the President's younger brother. He is still the youngest member of the Senate and remembers.

Ted had a better relationship with President Johnson than Bobby did, partly from his acceptance by the Senate inner club and partly because he had not sought Johnson's job. He doesn't hesitate to challenge Johnson, however. He has bitterly accused the administration of distorting Vietnam casualty figures.

His major mistake in the Senate was his backing at the ambassador's request of an old family friend, Francis X. Morrissey, for a federal judgeship. Morrissey's qualifications were questionable and it was Robert Kennedy who finally suggested that Ted drop his support. The younger brother did—with a sob of emotion in a dramatic floor speech.

One of Edward Kennedy's first major speeches in the Senate urged the outlawing of poll taxes. His brother, then a Senator from New York, wavered in his support for Ted's position and eventually decided not to.

Like Robert, Edward went to Harvard and then to the University of Virginia Law School. Ted had to work harder to get good grades than his brothers did.

He probably is a better athlete than they were.

Of the four sons, Ted was probably closest to the parents, especially to his mother, Rose.

It was Ted who told them of the assassination in Dallas. And it was Ted who had to tell them of the assassination in Los Angeles.

The Accused Assassin

Sirhan Sirhan may have been "inflamed" by
communists, according to Los Angeles mayor.

LOS ANGELES (UPI) . . . Mayor Sam Yorty has deduced that Sirhan Bishara Sirhan, accused assassin of Senator Robert F. Kennedy, had contacts with communist front groups.

"He was inflamed by contacts with the Communist party or communist-infiltrated organizations," Yorty told a Thursday news conference, his second on the subject of Sirhan in two days.

The mayor based his disclosures on two notebooks said to be found in Sirhan's home in suburban Pasadena. Neither the police department nor the state attorney general's office has confirmed the contents of the diary.

On Wednesday, Yorty told newsmen one of the notebooks contained the sentence: "Kennedy has to be assassinated before June 5, 1968"—the first anniversary of the six-day Israeli blitz in the Middle East.

Yorty said Thursday that investigators found that Sirhan's car, a pink DeSoto, was seen several times in front of the W. E. B. DuBois Club, labeled a communist front by the Justice Department.

"We have learned that his car was seen outside meetings where communist organizations or communist-front organizations were in session," Yorty said. "From that circumstance I guess we can deduce that he was in contact with organizations which were communist or sympathizers."

Pressed by newsmen, Yorty said Sirhan was never observed inside the DuBois club.

"But there is no question about his communist sympathy," he continued. "He clearly expressed his communist sympathy in his own writings (the notebooks)."

Investigators also are trying to determine whether Sirhan, an immigrant from Jordan, is linked with an Arab nationalist group.

"Arab nationalism also has now been inflamed by the communists,"

Yorty said, adding it would be consistent for Sirhan to be associated with both communists and Arab nationalists.

District Attorney Evelle J. Younger Thursday expressed concern during a news conference over release of information that might prejudice the case. He cautioned restraint on all evidentiary matters by the mayor, police, and newsmen.

Dorothy Healey, head of the Communist party in Southern California, said the DuBois club has not had a chapter here for more than a year. She said Yorty was attempting to "use this monstrous killing of Kennedy to his own political advantage in a most despicable way."

Yorty said he felt he was not prejudicing the case by his remarks.

"I don't see how you can prejudice a trial unless you make highly inflammatory statements," Yorty said. "There is always a question on the public's right to know and the question of revealing evidence. Because this happened in our city our people have a right to know a reasonable amount of background."

NBC correspondent Sander Vanocur, who traveled with the Kennedy family from Los Angeles with the Senator's body, said Thursday night the Kennedy family believed Yorty may have jeopardized the case against Sirhan by disclosing the contents of the alleged assassin's diary. Vanocur said the family also was upset by Yorty's appearance at the airport prior to the flight to New York and that the late Senator's press aide, Frank Mankiewicz, "diplomatically" asked the mayor to abandon his plans to see the Kennedys off. Yorty complied, the NBC correspondent said. Vanocur said the Kennedy family considered Yorty's appearance at the airport in questionable taste in view of a clash between Yorty and the late Senator at a Senate hearing following the Watts riots.

The stiff security cordon around Sirhan was tightened Thursday after the Los Angeles County sheriff received a barrage of death threats.

Eight to 12 telephone callers have threatened to shoot the accused assassin, bomb the county jail, and kill deputies guarding Sirhan, Sheriff Peter J. Pitchess told newsmen.

Sirhan is being held in an isolated second-floor cell on the remote hospital wing of the jail, the sheriff said, and is under constant surveillance by six uniformed guards. One deputy remains in the 24-square-foot cell with the suspect at all times. A second guard maintains a constant watch through an unbreakable glass porthole in the door. The square cell is painted gray and contains a bed, wash basin, and toilet. Four other deputies constantly guard a narrow corridor outside the cell. Five teams of two deputies each patrol the outer perimeter of the jail.

The sheriff said he has also increased patrols in the Pasadena neighborhood where Sirhan lived with his mother and two brothers.

Sirhan is incarcerated in the medical ward, the sheriff said, because he is under treatment for a broken left index finger and a sprained left ankle. He received the injuries, the sheriff said, "in the course of his arrest" at the Ambassador Hotel, in a struggle moments after Senator Kennedy was shot.

He is under the care of Dr. Marcus Crahan, the jail's medical director. Crahan also is a psychiatrist and Pitchess said the doctor "possibly" is giving the suspect psychiatric examination during the course of his treatment for the other injuries. The sheriff said Sirhan may be given an electroencephalogram, a brain-wave test used to detect brain damage.

Sirhan has made a "couple of requests" for special food, including orange juice and tuna fish, Pitchess said. These were recommended by doctors to quiet an upset stomach, "perhaps suffered from shock."

The prisoner, wearing regulation jail dress of blue denim trousers and shirt, spends most of his day "reclining on the cell bed," but is allowed to exercise in the company of two deputies by walking up and down the corridor, the sheriff said.

Pitchess said he did not know if the suspect was informed of Kennedy's death, but noted Sirhan "has access to newspapers."

The sheriff said he had not specifically told Sirhan that his life was threatened, but indicated in a general way that stiff security precautions were in effect. "I informed him that our responsibility was his security and we required his cooperation," Pitchess said. "We are more concerned about his outside safety than we are from him."

The first of many legal documents was being drafted Thursday in the state's drive to secure a first-degree murder conviction against Sirhan.

Deputy District Attorneys John Howard and Morio Fukuto will ask the 23-member county grand jury Friday to indict Sirhan on one murder charge and five counts of assault with intent to commit murder.

If convicted of first-degree murder, Sirhan could be sentenced to die in the San Quentin gas chamber at the gray-walled prison north of San Francisco. Two death row annexes presently house 77 inmates.

The jury also could send Sirhan, 24, to prison for life. The Jordanian immigrant could ask to be paroled after serving seven years of a life term. The California Adult Authority is the agency which determines when or if an inmate is released.

Each charge of assault with intent to commit murder carries a sentence of life in prison. The life term is set by statute rather than the jury. If a second-degree murder conviction were returned, the sentence—again determined by statute—also is life in prison.

In Washington, the Justice Department said Warren Christopher, Deputy U.S. Attorney General, had gone to Los Angeles to "assure that every investigative resource is brought to bear on every possible aspect of the case and that federal agencies provide all possible assistance to local authorities."

Two books on the mystical doctrine of theosophy were delivered to the cell of Sirhan Thursday at his request.

The accused assassin was raised in a Greek Orthodox family in Palestine but occasionally attended the Westminster Presbyterian Church near the family home in Pasadena.

One of the books, *Talks On, 'At the Feet of the Master,'* by the Rt. Rev. C. W. Leadbeater, was described as a book a penitent person might want to read.

The other, *The Secret Doctrine,* by Madame Helena Petrovna Blavatsky, is one of a five-volume series published in 1888. Madame Blavatsky, a Russian princess, was one of the founders of the Theosophical Society in 1875.

Theosophy borrows from the philosophy of the Hindu religion without adopting the external forms of Hindu worship. It is universalist in nature, teaching that God is present in all things.

It aimed through its societies to serve as a nucleus as the universal brotherhood of man and attainment of perfection through the study of universal laws. It taught physical and spiritual evolution, as of the soul through reincarnation.

One passage in Madame Blavatsky's book reads:

"There would be no life possible (in our world of illusions) without death nor regeneration and reconstruction without destruction."

Information gathered by newsmen pictured Sirhan as a young man passionately pro-Arab who was not happy in America. He was born March 19, 1944, in the Armenian section of the old walled city of Jerusalem, then under Jordanian control. He was the fourth of five boys born to Bishara and Mary Sirhan, who were Greek Orthodox Christians.

On Jan. 12, 1957, when he was 12 years old, he arrived in New York with his father, mother, and a number of brothers and a sister. His father returned to Jerusalem after a short period, but the other Sirhans moved to California.

Sirhan graduated from high school in Pasadena, went to junior college and then began drifting from job to job. As far as is known, he never had any previous contact with the law.

Most of his friends, fellow workers, and neighbors found him a nice enough fellow but said he was passionately pro-Arab.

"When there was trouble between Jordan and Israel, he would become inflamed," said John Shear, who worked with Sirhan at Hollywood Park race track. "Since I wasn't interested in politics, I would not discuss it but he was violently pro-Jordan and anti-Israel."

In other cities, former Pasadena classmates of the accused assassin described the boy from a broken home as a quiet, brilliant youth who kept to himself.

In Saigon, Lt. William A. Spaniard, 24, of Pasadena, recalled Sirhan was "a taciturn individual who did not say very much. Friendly, really pleasant, but hard to get to know."

"He was brilliant. He was studying Russian when everyone else was barely getting by in Spanish and English," the officer said.

Christian Ek, 23, a Swede who also was a classmate of Sirhan, said in Stockholm the young Arab "dreamed of being something big in Jordan after his studies in the United States. He was a calm, well-mannered boy, nothing evil about him."

The family of Sirhan Sirhan had a reputation in Jerusalem of being "pious and devoted people," an Armenian churchman said Thursday in New York.

Bishop Shahe Ajamian, diplomatic envoy of the Armenian patriarch of Jerusalem, said Sirhan's father, a civil servant in charge of the water supply in the Jordanian sector of the city, was "not at all the type of fanatic, emotional person."

Ajamian said the "psychological background" for Sirhan's alleged attack upon Kennedy "must be found in the profound hate created between the Arabs and Israel."

People in the tiny Christian village of Teibeh in Israeli-occupied Jordan, where Sirhan Sirhan grew up, found it difficult to believe that he could have assassinated Robert Kennedy.

"A very gentle, polite, quiet and humble boy, interested mainly in books" said a schoolteacher of the Arab boy who left for America a decade ago and came back in headlines that shocked Teibeh.

Salim Awad, the principal of the village's Lutheran school, said, "It is beyond comprehension how he could have committed such a terrible act on his own initiative without having been put up to do this by some other people."

The village elder, Faiz Ba'Ajis Muaddi, also said there must have been someone behind Sirhan's actions.

The Arab elders expressed the conviction Sirhan could not have committed the crime "unless he was influenced or offered a lot of money."

Arabs in East Jerusalem where the family had lived were bitter to suggestions Sirhan hated Kennedy for supporting Israel against Jordan.

"He's been living in America for 11 years. Why does he want to involve us?" demanded hotel owner Mohammed Khalik.

In Cairo, newspapers gave their own explanations.

Al Ahram, often the semi-official voice of the Egyptian government, said Kennedy's assassination was a "terrible tragedy." It called Sirhan "a natural product of the atmosphere of violence in America. He has been away from his Arab homeland for 11 years—since the time he was 12—and these were decisive years in his mental and psychological growth . . .

"Although heavy on the heart, it nevertheless has to be said . . . that American discrimination against the Arabs acts as pressure on the nerves, particularly the nerves of Arab emigrants to America."

Bishara Sirhan, 52-year-old father of the accused assassin, lives in the village of Teibeh in Israeli-occupied Jordan.

Sirhan's Father

"If my son did it, he deserves his fate."

by Eliav Simon

TEIBEH, ISRAELI-OCCUPIED JORDAN (UPI) . . . The small gray-haired man kept shrugging his shoulders as he stood Thursday before his modest stone house in this sun-baked sleepy Christian village.

"I'm stupefied. I'm shocked. This is the blackest day of my life," said Bishara Sirhan. "I pray to the Almighty that this nightmare may pass."

Sirhan and his small village, as ancient as the Bible, became linked today with a world-stunning deed in faraway Los Angeles. An elder from the village, Faiz Ba'Ajis Muaddi, hurried to Sirhan's two-story house to tell him his fourth son, Sirhan, 24, had been charged with the assassination of Robert Kennedy.

"If my son did it, he deserves his fate," said the 52-year-old Sirhan, his lips quivering. "I always have had such deep admiration for the Kennedy family."

For a moment the father was silent in the summer sunshine. Then he looked up at his interviewer. His gray-green eyes blazed.

"How do you expect me to know why he shot Robert Kennedy?" he demanded.

Staring at the horizon as if talking to himself, he said, "My son was a talented boy, more than his four brothers. How he came to this is beyond me."

The accused assassin came from a religious Christian family. He was born in Jerusalem and the family of seven lived in the Armenian quarter. Young Sirhan went to a Lutheran school and the father said the family belonged to the Greek Orthodox Church.

"I am a religious man and have been all my life," said Bishara Sirhan. "I still am a steady churchgoer and read the Bible every day. My son as a child used to go to the Orthodox Church with me in Jerusalem every Sunday. We studied the Bible together."

The father worked for the British army during World War II at the city water supply and speaks nearly unaccented English. The family emigrated to the United States in 1957 but the quarreling parents separated and the father returned alone to his native land. He said he lives on a "very small" retirement pension, works part time on his small farm land "and need no help."

The father said he last saw his son three years ago on a visit to the United States.

Teibeh village is built on several hills about 30 miles north of Jerusalem. Three handsome stone Orthodox and Roman Catholic Churches on three hills testify to the times when the congregations were prosperous.

The father slipped an old tweed jacket over his white nylon shirt and bright blue tie and said, "I am very tired." He turned and walked slowly, heavily, to a cafe in the village to escape a crowd of newsmen that descended on Teibeh.

Assassination Conspiracy?

Police hunt for mystery woman in polka dot dress accused of saying, "We shot him!" after Kennedy shooting.

LOS ANGELES (UPI) . . . Police said today they had issued an all points bulletin for a possible woman suspect in the assassination of Senator Robert F. Kennedy.

The bulletin was issued after a Kennedy campaign worker told police that a woman in a polka dot dress ran from the Ambassador Hotel early Wednesday at about the time an assassin fired eight shots at Kennedy.

"We shot him," Miss Sandy Serrano said the woman told her.

Police described the woman in their bulletin as a white female, 23 to 27 years old, 5-foot-6, wearing a white voile dress with three-quarter sleeves, and small black polka dots.

Miss Serrano, a 20-year-old Youth for Kennedy worker from nearby Pasadena, explained in a television interview after the shooting that she had gone out on a hotel terrace as Kennedy began his speech claiming victory in Tuesday's California Democratic Presidential primary.

"A girl came running down the steps and said, 'We shot him!'" Miss Serrano said. A man allegedly was with the girl.

"Who did you shoot? Who did you shoot?" Miss Serrano said she asked.

"'We shot Senator Kennedy,'" was the answer, she reported.

Miss Serrano said she had seen the pair earlier in the evening with another man, but the latter was not with them when they left the hotel.

Meanwhile, in New York, state police alerted all law enforcement officers in the state to be on the lookout for "eight Quebec revolutionists" reported to be on their way from Canada to avenge the slaying of Senator Robert F. Kennedy.

The alert bulletin that went to all police departments said the would-be assassins had selected as their targets President Johnson, Vice President Hubert H. Humphrey, and New York Governor Nelson A. Rockefeller.

The tip that the men were on their way into New York from Canada came in an anonymous telephone call to the American Consulate in Montreal, police said. State police, who did not have a description of the eight, were watching all border crossings for suspicious persons.

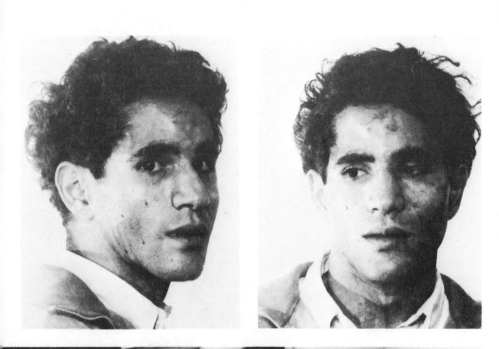

Second-hand .22-caliber revolver used in the assassination of Robert Kennedy is shown here with the police "mug shots" of the accused assassin Sirhan Bishara Sirhan.

Assassin's Weapon

*Original owner bought it
for "protection" after Watts riots.*

LOS ANGELES (UPI) . . . The snub-nosed revolver used to shoot Senator Robert F. Kennedy passed through the hands of at least four persons since it was first purchased about the time of the Watts riots in 1965.

Despite its roundabout journey into the possession of the suspected assailant, the .22-caliber Iver Johnson "Cadet" pistol was identified in a matter of seconds from the 2.5 million registered weapons in California.

State Attorney General Thomas C. Lynch said a new computer at the Bureau of Criminal Investigation and Identification in Sacramento plucked it out of the records "just seconds" after police supplied the serial number.

The eight-shot weapon was wrested early Wednesday from Sirhan Bishara Sirhan, who settled in suburban Pasadena about five years ago.

The official records on the revolver begin in 1965 when it was bought by Albert L. Hertz, 72, Alhambra, for home protection during the August, 1965, racial violence in Watts. He gave it to his daughter, Mrs. Robert F. Westlake, 35, who then lived in Pasadena, for her protection.

"I didn't want the gun lying around the house with two small children here," she said. So she gave it to her next door neighbor, George Charles Erhard, 18. She later moved to Woodacre, a Marin County community north of San Francisco, and it was there she was called by authorities to inquire about the ownership of the weapon.

Mrs. Westlake telephoned Erhard, who told her he had sold the gun.

Police Chief Tom Reddin said Erhard told police he sold the gun "to a bushy-haired guy named Joe," whom officers later identified as the suspect's brother, Munir Sirhan.

"Joe" Sirhan told officers he had no idea how the weapon had fallen into the hands of his brother. Mrs. Westlake said, "I'd have been better off if I'd burned the darned thing."

117

New Protection for Candidates

Congress and President act to provide
Secret Service guards for politicians

by Merriman Smith

WASHINGTON (UPI) . . . Bereaved and indignant at the assassination of Robert F. Kennedy, Congress and President Johnson have moved quickly to provide what they hope will be insurance against further political murder.

The President Thursday signed into law legislation authorizing Secret Service protection of major candidates for the Presidency and Vice Presidency.

The House and Senate acted within hours of Kennedy's death to approve the protection. Johnson, acting extralegally, already had dispatched federal agents to protect all major candidates after Kennedy's shooting in Los Angeles.

Secret Service men are now protecting Senator Eugene J. McCarthy, former Vice President Richard M. Nixon, New York Governor Nelson A. Rockefeller, Harold Stassen, and third-party candidate George A. Wallace. Vice President Hubert H. Humphrey, the leading Democratic contender for the Presidential nomination, already has such protection.

The legislation speedily approved Thursday legalized Johnson's action of the day before and provided $400,000 to finance protection of the candidates through the end of this month.

Next week, legislation is expected to provide an extra $2 million to the Secret Service for the upcoming fiscal year.

There are currently 575 trained Secret Service agents. In addition to protecting the President and Vice President, the agents are charged with enforcing laws against counterfeiting and forgery of government checks and bonds.

The White House said if there are not enough Secret Service agents to protect all the candidates, agents will be borrowed from the FBI, the Internal Revenue Service, the Narcotics Bureau, the Customs Bureau and, on occasion, from the military and local law enforcement agencies.

In addition to protecting the Chief Executive and the Vice President, secret service agents provide security for past Presidents and Mrs. John F. Kennedy and her children.

Such protection to the candidates might not have saved Senator Kennedy's life, according to Senator A. S. Mike Monroney, D-Okla., who managed the security bill. But he said he was sure the government guards, with their special training, probably would have secured the area where the Senator was shot.

For security reasons, the Treasury Department refused to divulge how many agents have been assigned to the candidates. Any of the candidates, under the legislation passed Thursday, can refuse federal protection, but none has.

The Treasury said the number of guards would vary, depending upon the individual candidate's travels and amount of security required by local conditions. Six agents showed up at Nixon's apartment in New York shortly after the President decided to provide such protection early Wednesday.

Under the legislation, the Treasury Secretary—who controls the Secret Service—would decide who qualified for protection, in consultation with a bipartisan congressional advisory committee.

The involved and sometimes impossible problems of protecting a person in high public office were underlined by the shooting of Robert F. Kennedy in the kitchen corridor of a Los Angeles hotel.

Kennedy had minimal protection from a few husky staff members. But his brother, John F. Kennedy, believed there was no airtight protection even for a chief executive when a potential assassin was prepared to give his own life in exchange.

The U.S. Secret Service, charged by law with responsibility for the safety of the President, can protect their charge only to the extent that the Chief Executive is willing to cooperate.

This same condition will apply for the rest of this campaign year as the Secret Service attempts to safeguard the Presidential candidates.

Agents assigned to protect Presidential candidates undoubtedly will run into problems as they form protective cordons around their man in crowds, as they take him out of hotels via secret routes, and inspect all packages addressed to his home or hotel.

But what happened to Robert F. Kennedy might make tight security a bit more acceptable to the candidates, and make them feel a bit more comfortable.

The United States, compared with other theoretically civilized nations, has perhaps the worst assassination record of modern history. Yet, in the face of this, Presidents insist on exposing themselves to the public under conditions which are less than ideal for their well-being.

Should a President submit to near-perfect precautions, he would have to become a recluse of 1600 Pennsylvania Avenue. Even there, persons admitted to his presence would have to be checked and searched to assure his complete safety.

He would have to forgo virtually all public appearances outside the White House; travel without any public announcement whatever, and give up almost any form of surface travel. This would confine movement to helicopters and heavily guarded aircraft.

What the Secret Service had had to do thus far is live with compromise, for no President wants to appear in such fear of his safety that he forgoes all open contact with his fellow countrymen.

Partly because of the John F. Kennedy assassination, which occurred during an open-car procession through Dallas on Nov. 22, 1963, Johnson now moves on city streets only in a closed, armored vehicle with thick bullet-proof windows.

When he does participate in a motorcade through a city, the procession usually moves at a rate of 30 miles per hour or more on the theory that vehicular speed is a protection against would-be riflemen who might be hiding in nearby office buildings.

At least one helicopter usually hovers ahead of and over a Presidential motorcade with a specially trained agent watching for hidden vehicles which might try to interdict the parade—or for simple traffic jams which might bring the procession to a halt.

When President Johnson goes to a hotel banquet in Washington or out of town, a sizable job of Secret Service research is involved. The record of every hotel employee who might be in proximity to the Chief Executive must be checked. If one who will be working close to the President turns out to have a police record of violence, he usually is excused from work during the Presidential visit.

From the Secret Service standpoint, there is good and bad in a President's decision to move suddenly and without warning. The favorable aspect is a matter of surprise. The negative side of sudden, surprise movement is the lack of time for advance precautions.

Congress Passes Gun Control Bill

New measure would ban mail sale of hand guns, but President calls for tougher restrictions.

by Ann Wood

WASHINGTON (UPI) . . . Spurred by the Kennedy assassination, the House passed and sent to the White House Thursday a bill containing limited firearm controls, but President Johnson at once pleaded with Congress for the far broader restrictions on all gun sales that Senator Edward M. Kennedy proposed three weeks ago.

Just after the House approved by a vote of 368-17 the anticrime bill with its restrictions on the sale of pistols and revolvers, the Chief Executive went on television and asked for a stronger measure "in the name of sanity."

He sought the gun sales restrictions that Kennedy had proposed as an amendment to the crime bill when it was in the Senate. Kennedy's measure, extending the controls to cover rifles and shotguns, was defeated 53-29 on May 16. The bill approved by both houses imposes limits only on the sale of hand guns.

President Johnson said, "Surely this must be clear without question: The hour has come for the Congress to enact a strong and effective gun control law, governing the full range of lethal weapons.

"I call upon the Congress in the name of sanity, in the name of safety —and in the name of an aroused nation—to give America the gun control law it needs."

Pickets march in front of National Rifle Association Headquarters in Washington, D.C., demanding stricter gun control laws.

After the President spoke, the House adopted a resolution deploring the slaying of Senator Robert F. Kennedy by an assassin who carried a hand gun. Then members adjourned.

The future of the bill was in question not only because of its moderate curbs on gun sales but also because of sections authorizing wiretapping and over-ruling Supreme Court decisions.

The bill passed by the House today provided the first new federal gun controls in 30 years. Effective in 180 days, the crime control measure would ban mail order sales of hand guns, limit store sales to adult residents of the state, and curb traffic in imported firearms and military-type weapons.

The bill sets forth specifications that foreign military surplus weapons must meet to qualify as being suitable for sporting uses or as collectors' items. Those that do not meet these specifications would be prohibited from entering this country, unless made exceptions through a special ruling by the Treasury Secretary.

To improve local police forces, the bill authorizes a $400 million, two-year program of aid that is subject to later appropriation of the money in separate legislation.

Two other sections were opposed by liberals and the administration as infringing on individual rights of privacy and due process of law.

One would permit court-supervised wiretapping in investigating major crime and in national security cases, but forbid it in other circumstances.

The second, aimed at strengthening the prosecutor's hand by upsetting recent Supreme Court rulings, would broaden the admissibility of confessions and eyewitness testimony in court trials. Liberals warned that the High Court itself might throw this out.

The measure permits trial judges to determine if a confession was given voluntarily or if eyewitness testimony was admissible, but each decision would be subject to review by the Supreme Court.

Despite reservations, Johnson would find it difficult to veto the bill in a political election year marked by peaking violence capped with the assassinations of Kennedy and of the Reverend Martin Luther King.

The tide for the bill was demonstrated by the sweeping vote of House members, who said the nation demanded that Congress "do something about crime and violence now."

The Senate pieced the bill together in weeks of debate before passing it 72-4. Just hours after Kennedy was shot, the House rejected, 317-60, a move to send it to a joint conference for modifications.

The only federal gun control laws now on the books were enacted in 1934 and 1938 to limit traffic in gangster weapons such as sawed-off shotguns and machine guns, prohibit interstate shipments to felons, and require federal licensing of interstate dealers.

Despite the swell of support for the crime control bill in the wake of Kennedy's slaying, nobody suggested that it would have saved him. But many said his death underscored the need for action against a national crisis of crime and violence.

Kennedy in fact was on record as being dissatisfied with portions of the bill. He favored aid to police, but wanted it to go directly to local forces rather than through state governments. He wanted stronger gun controls covering rifles and shotguns, opposed provisions aimed at the Supreme Court, and felt the provisions allowing wiretapping were too broad. Off campaigning much of the time, Kennedy did not vote on final Senate passage.

Specifically, the President asked Congress to prohibit the mail order sale of rifles and shotguns; prohibit the sale of long guns to anyone under the age of 18, and to prohibit over-the-counter sales of rifles and long guns to any purchaser who does not live in the same state as the dealer.

The President said that his recommendations would not prevent legitimate hunters or sportsmen from purchasing firearms but it would give the individual states proper incentive to shape their own gun control legislation.

President Johnson's Appeal For Stronger Gun Laws

The text of the statement by President Johnson calling on Congress to enact more restrictive gun control laws follows:

Today the nation cries out to the conscience of the Congress. Criminal violence from the muzzle of a gun has once again brought heartbreak to America. Surely this must be clear beyond question: The hour has come for the Congress to enact a strong and effective gun control law governing the full range of lethal weapons.

I have sought and I have fought for such a law through all the days of my Presidency. On many occasions before, I have spoken of the terrible toll inflicted on our people by firearms—750,000 Americans dead since the turn of the century.

This is far more than have died at the hands of all of our enemies in all of the wars that we have fought—sorrow and suffering that just cannot be counted and fear that can never be measured.

Each year in this country, guns are involved in more than 6,500 murders. This compares with 30 in England, 99 in Canada, 68 in West Germany and 37 in Japan.

Forty-four thousand aggravated assaults are committed with guns in America each year. Fifty thousand robberies are committed with guns in America each year.

I have told the Congress and I have told the nation of the brutal loophole in our nation's laws. Two million guns were sold in the United States last year. Far too many of those guns were bought by the demented and the deranged, the hardened criminal and the convict, the addict and the alcoholic.

And we cannot expect these irresponsible people to be prudent in their protection of us. But we can and we have a right to expect the Congress of the United States to protect us from them.

Weapons of destruction can be purchased by mail as easily as baskets of fruit or cartons of cigarettes.

We must eliminate the dangers of mail-order murder in this country.

The Congress has finally begun to take some action. The Senate has passed a watered-down version of the gun control law I sent to the Congress some time ago with my recommendations.

The House has taken action on the Senate bill. But this halfway measure is not near enough. It covers adequately only transactions involving hand guns. It leaves the deadly commerce in lethal shotguns and rifles without effective control 55 long months after the mail-order murder of President John F. Kennedy.

So today I call upon the Congress in the name of sanity. I call upon the Congress in the name of safety and in the name of an aroused citizenship to give America the gun control law that American citizens need.

I urge the Congress to make it unlawful to sell rifles and shotguns as well as hand guns by mail order. I urge the Congress to make it unlawful to sell rifles and shotguns as well as hand guns to persons who are too young to bear the terrible responsibility that is placed in the hands of a gun owner.

I urge the Congress and plead with it to make it unlawful to sell rifles and shotguns as well as hand guns in one state to the residents of another state.

This will not prevent legitimate hunters or sportsmen from purchasing firearms, but with this reinforced law we can then give the states the proper incentive to shape their own gun control legislation and the country can at long last have a network of systematic safeguards for all of our citizens.

And today I am asking each of the Governors of the 50 states to immediately and to comprehensively review their gun laws and to amend them where necessary and rewrite them in order to fully protect the citizens of the states that they serve, protect them from the deadly weapons that are now in dangerous hands.

The voices of the few must no longer prevail over the interest of the many. When I last appealed to the Congress on this subject again—and that was only a month ago—I asked this question: What in the name of conscience will it take to pass a truly effective gun control law in the Congress.

And now in this new hour of tragedy that question should at last be answered.

So let us now spell out our grief in constructive action.

Flowers for a friend. Children bring bouquet and sympathy note to the Kennedy home in McLean, Va.

The World Sorrows

*Around the world men weep and
lament the future of the United States.*

by Frank Swoboda

WASHINGTON (UPI) . . . President Johnson proclaimed Sunday a national day of mourning for Senator Robert F. Kennedy and asked Americans to "walk together through this dark night of common anguish into a new dawn of healing unity."

He ordered the flag flown at half-staff at U.S. government and military installations at home and abroad until after the requiem mass is said and the assassinated New York Senator is buried on Saturday at Arlington National Cemetery.

Vice President Hubert H. Humphrey received special permission as presiding officer in the Senate to deliver a "statement of respect and affection to the life and memory" of Kennedy.

In a voice quaking with emotion, Humphrey said after a day of eulogies on the floor that the nation must "dispel the force of unreason and hate, extremism and violence in our midst." Kennedy, he said, was "taken from us by an irrational act of hatred while doing the most sacred work of free men."

At 5:01 a.m.—17 minutes after Kennedy died in Los Angeles—White House assistant Walt W. Rostow telephoned Johnson with the news. "Mr. President," he said, "it has just been announced that Senator Kennedy has died."

A short time later the President made this statement:

"This is a time of tragedy and loss. Senator Robert Kennedy is dead.

"Robert Kennedy affirmed this country—affirmed the essential decency

129

of its people, their longing for peace, their desire to improve conditions of life for all.

"During his life, he knew far more than his share of personal tragedy.

"Yet he never abandoned his faith in America. He never lost his confidence in the spiritual strength of ordinary men and women. He believed in the capacity of the young for excellence—and in the right of the old and poor to a life of dignity.

"Our public life is diminished by his loss.

"Mrs. Johnson and I extend our deepest sympathy to Mrs. Kennedy and his family. I have issued a proclamation calling upon our nation to observe a day of mourning for Robert Kennedy."

Among the other outpourings of sorrow was a poignant question asked by the widow of Martin Luther King, who was felled by a sniper two months ago.

"As my husband and Senator Kennedy kept warning the nation, we must put an end to violence or violence would put an end to us," she said in Los Angeles. "Once again I ask the question: How many husbands, how many fathers and how many sons must die before we as men, women, youths and children—before we as a nation—will rise up in righteous indignation and demand an end to such senseless violence?"

In the gloom of the Senate chamber, Kennedy's desk was bare. Senate Democratic leader Mike Mansfield, who delivered a eulogy to the late President at the Capitol in 1963, rose again and asked: "What in the name of God has happened to us?"

The Senate adopted a resolution expressing its "profound sorrow and deep regret" and went on to approve Johnson's request for Secret Service protection for all major candidates for Presidential nomination and their families.

It was a break in long-standing tradition for the Senate to conduct business the day one of its members dies, but Mansfield said Kennedy's family had told him, "this is what Bob would like to have done."

Mansfield said a sizable delegation of Senators would fly to New York Saturday and return on the train that will carry Kennedy's body to Washington for burial.

The President made four of his fleet of air force planes available to the Kennedy family, including one Boeing 707 to carry the Senator's body to New York City for lying in state.

In Washington, a special low mass was said in Kennedy's memory at St. Matthew's Cathedral, where his brother's funeral service was held. Patrick Cardinal O'Boyle will celebrate another mass there Friday and called for memorial services in every local parish on Sunday.

Walter E. Washington, the District's Negro mayor, ordered flags flown at half-staff. The Washington Senators baseball team cancelled a scheduled game Saturday with the Minnesota Twins.

Many of the expressions of mourning from Capitol Hill mentioned lawlessness and violence sweeping the country. But Secretary of State Dean Rusk said, "We must not indict an entire people because of the wanton acts of certain violent individuals."

In a statement, Rusk said, "The American people are a decent, wholesome, generous and dedicated people who want to establish peace in the world and equality and social justice here at home." He added that both slain Kennedys would expect the nation to take on its unfinished business "with all the wisdom and energy we can possibly muster."

Robert S. McNamara, the World Bank president whom the late President chose as his Defense Secretary, cancelled talks with bank officials in Frankfurt, Germany, and flew back for Kennedy's funeral. A McNamara visit to Indonesia Saturday was postponed until next week.

Sen. Eugene J. McCarthy, D-Minn., who had rivaled Kennedy for the Democratic Presidential nomination, said words alone could not ease the Kennedy family's anguish.

"Let us seek to comfort them by our quiet mourning, our rejection of violence and reprisal and by offering renewed dedication to the cause of peace and reconciliation which Robert Kennedy served," he said.

In New York, Governor Nelson A. Rockefeller ordered flags on all state buildings flown at half-staff to mark what he called "an unspeakable tragedy and a terrible loss to the nation."

Richard M. Nixon, the governor's chief opponent for the Republican Presidential nomination, said Kennedy's death was a "terrible tragedy both for a family and a nation which have known too many such tragedies in recent times."

———————

Nixon said the tragedy of Kennedy's assassination "would be compounded if we were to allow the shock of this event to cause us to lose confidence in ourselves or our nation."

"The greatest legacy of Robert F. Kennedy and John F. Kennedy was this: Two men who could have comfortably sat on the sidelines plunged into the arena of public service with a zest, a vigor, a spirit which inspired millions to follow their example," Nixon said.

The former Vice President, in answer to critics who have described the assassination as an indication of national illness, said: "There are sick people in America, but the American people are not a sick nation."

"Senator Kennedy had an answer for those who might have contended otherwise," Nixon said. "Among his last words were these: 'America is a great nation. America is a strong nation. America is a compassionate nation with an unfinished agenda of business at home and abroad.'"

Tears on his cheeks and a lump in his throat, Harold Macmillan asked his fellow Britons to show a little understanding for their American cousins.

The 74-year-old former Prime Minister, addressing a nation shocked by the assassination of Senator Robert F. Kennedy, said harsh, wrong things were being said about America and its people.

"What is the American people? What are they? They are our people, who went out from this island, all refugees, all persecuted.

"The Catholics to Maryland, the dissenters to New England, because at home they couldn't hold their faith and live their lives," he said during a nationally televised speech.

"More and more people came, but many of them refugees too from all over Europe. Now they are even from Asia."

Tears ran down his cheeks. Macmillan, who had known Kennedy well, fought to control his voice. His mother had been an American. He wanted no misunderstanding.

"So America is this vast continent, this huge population which hasn't yet, as it were, settled down into the melting pot. . . . It has problems. It is a frontier line still."

Macmillan said his mother, the late Helen Belles of Indiana, used to "pull down the blinds every night when the sun went down . . . it was her tradition because the Indians were on the other side of the river looking into the house.

"So let us be fair about America. They've got this enormous problem of population, this great wealth, this great technique. But it is a world of its own. It is Europe and part of Asia now, planted in the New World."

Macmillan said Britons should show not only "sympathy, sorrow, but determination to understand, to help, to work with them."

In Moscow Russian poet Yevgeny Yevtushenko mourned Senator Robert F. Kennedy in verse.

The two men had met and talked together during Yevtushenko's most recent American tour. Despite this, the poem which the aging "angry young man" of Soviet poetry read on Moscow television was often more propagandistic than personal.

It linked Kennedy's death with the war in Vietnam. And its title, "The Freedom to Kill," repeated the theme of the Soviet press to the slaying. Addressing the United States, Yevtushenko said:

"You promised to be the conscience of the world,
"But beside the shameful abyss
"You are not shooting at (Martin Luther) King
"But at your own conscience.
"You are bombing Vietnam, and along with this,
"You are bombing your honor.
"So rise stricken Statue of Liberty
"And condemn the freedom to kill."

In London grim-faced Prime Minister Harold Wilson expressed outrage at Senator Robert F. Kennedy's assassination and urged Britons and Americans to reaffirm their faith in democracy.

Wilson, in an emotional nationwide television statement, warned under-privileged minorities will turn to "violent solutions" unless racial, political, and religious hatreds are eliminated.

"This senseless and brutal murder has touched the hearts and outraged the minds of all of us in Britain," Wilson said. "Every family here mourns with Robert Kennedy's widow, with his children and with his parents."

"But it is not only a tragedy for one family or one nation," Wilson said. "It is a tragedy in which we are all involved. For the bullets which struck down Robert Kennedy were a symptom of the attacks which in country after country, and in varying forms, are being aimed at democracy itself."

Wilson said that "what we are now seeing is violence bred by enemies of democracy, impatient with the way it works—and with violence created, too, by cynicism and apathy in the working of democracy."

"It is for us," Wilson said, "to ensure by our response to his death that the seeking after violent solutions, the stirring of hatred against a man because of his race, because of his religion or because of his political convictions whatever they may be, that these evil things should be out-lawed from our great democracies. That because a man has died in the assertion of democracy we should not ourselves, the living, become cyni-cal about democracy and liberty."

The British Prime Minister warned that "what we cannot do, what we must not do, is to allow the causes for which such men have fought to be lost—be it through apathy, cowardice or compromise."

He said that "if the sense of horror of all our people is as real as I believe it to be, then we must join with the leaders of American democracy in the resolve that this time a Kennedy shall not have died in vain."

Soviet Premier Alexei Kosygin deplored the "villainous assassination" of Senator Robert F. Kennedy in a telegram to the Senator's widow.

Kosygin said: "Allow me to express my sincere condolences over the grave loss befallen you and your family. The villainous assassination of your husband, Robert F. Kennedy, arouses the feeling of profound indignation of the Soviet people."

The Soviet Parliament sent a telegram to Vice President Hubert H. Humphrey, President of the Senate, saying, "The atrocious crime to which Robert Kennedy fell victim arouses indignation of the Soviet people."

The telegram to Humphrey was signed by Ivan Spiridonov, chairman of the Soviet of the Union of the Supreme Soviet, and Justas Paleckis, chairman of the Soviet of Nationalities of the Supreme Soviet.

Canadian Prime Minister Pierre Elliott Trudeau, terming the death of Robert F. Kennedy "a blow to all of us," sent a message of "deepest sympathy" to his widow and President Lyndon Johnson.

"I'm sure that all Canadians share my grief at the sad news of the death of Mr. Robert Kennedy," the Prime Minister said. "To his wife and to his family, and to the American people, I extend our deepest sympathy.

"The Canadian people feel very close to them in this sad hour, this hour of trial.

"Senator Kennedy devoted his life to the service of his fellow citizens. His death will be a blow to all those who shared his views . . . to the millions who benefited from his services. He worked for the underprivileged and for those who were in distress.

"His death is a blow to all of us but we will try to continue working for the values for which he stood."

In California, Governor Ronald Reagan ordered an official state of mourning for California to last through the funeral of Senator Robert F. Kennedy with all flags in the state be kept at half-staff through the mourning period.

His official statement said:

"The tragic, senseless death of Senator Kennedy affects all Californians and all Americans. My sympathies go out to Mrs. Kennedy and the Senator's children, as well as his parents and other members of his family. The prayers of all Americans are with them.

"I have declared a state of mourning for California to extend through the Senator's funeral and directed that all flags in California be flown at half-staff during the period of mourning."

In Boston, Richard Cardinal Cushing, drawing parallels in the lives and deaths of President John F. Kennedy and his younger brother Robert, said the death of Robert F. Kennedy "rends the heart of America already scarred by earlier sorrow."

The Roman Catholic Archbishop of Boston, a long-time Kennedy family friend, was with former Ambassador and Mrs. Joseph P. Kennedy at their Hyannis Port home on Cape Cod Wednesday before returning late at night to his archdiocesan residence here.

He learned of Kennedy's death on a radio newscast, the Cardinal said.

"The madness of men once again grieves our nation and brings us to our knees in prayer," he said. "We have lost another of our sons in the promise of his youth and the vigor of his years."

He said the Senator "displayed a kind of courage rare in any generation."

"Like his brother, he did not know the meaning of fear," the Cardinal said. "Where fear was wedded to danger, he embraced it.

"Today he is with God. Our prayers are offered for him. The Lord summoned him in the city named for the queens of angels. May those angels make room now to welcome him."

In San Francisco, Mayor Joseph Alioto set aside a week in July for any San Franciscan to turn in any kind of gun at his neighborhood police station or firehouse. He said no questions would be asked.

"I know of no greater way of commemorating Senator Kennedy than by this positive act," Alioto told a news conference.

"I have confidence, because of the great communications we have (with minority groups), that there will be no danger in turning in the guns."

Alioto said the weeklong gun "moratorium" would begin July 4, a Thursday. He made a specific appeal to the city's youth and mothers who have young men in their homes. He said the registration of any guns turned in would not be traced, and that no questions of any kind would be asked.

The mayor said he was not concerned with hunting rifles or guns designed for target shooting, but with small weapons that can be concealed.

Alioto also urged that legislation be passed at every level of government to control guns. He said Congress "should start the machinery at once to amend the Constitution" so it would preserve the rights of citizens to protect themselves, but at the same time provide effective gun controls.

In Los Angeles, the family of Senator Kennedy's accused assassin sent a brief telegram to the Kennedy family which expressed sadness and remorse.

"It hurts us very bad what has happened. It hurts everybody very much I am crying for them all," said the telegram, which was signed "Mrs. Mary Sirhan and family."

The family of the accused assassin, Sirhan Sirhan, reportedly was taken from their Pasadena home to another city under police protection.

In Claremont, Calif., Mrs. Medgar Evers, who also lost her husband to an assassin's bullet, expressed her grief over the death of Senator Robert F. Kennedy in a telegram to his widow.

Mrs. Evers, the widow of the slain Mississippi civil rights leader, said: "The family of Medgar Evers shares with you profound grief and deep loss. As my daughter, Rena, and I talked and shared with you and Senator Kennedy, the many miles in Atlanta (at the funeral of Dr. Martin Luther King Jr., also an assassination victim) only a few weeks ago, there were expressions between us of concern, faith and hope for a better America. Senator Kennedy gave us that hope and through the example that he, President John Kennedy, Martin Luther King Jr. and Medgar Evers gave, I pray that we as a nation learn from them. Our prayers are with you."

In Washington, the Rev. Ralph David Abernathy, leader of the Poor People's Campaign, urged President Johnson's new commission on violence in America to begin its work by studying "oppression, fear, greed, racism, poverty and warfare."

These, he said, are the "stark and formidable reality" which lead to violence.

Abernathy said the assassination of Senator Robert F. Kennedy "is one of the most infamous and sinister acts of violence in America" but it was also a "manifestation of violence which the nation permits."

Hosea Williams, leader of demonstrations, said the poor would shift their focus for a few days, changing from protest marches to street prayer vigils against "violence and hatred." He said clergymen would be recruited from Washington area churches to read scriptures and sermons at the demonstrations.

"Due to the loss of one of the greatest men of our time," Williams told newsmen at Resurrection City, the demonstrators will concentrate on protesting "the hatred and violence that is destroying all of us."

In Philadelphia, U.S. District Judge A. Leon Higginbotham Jr. said the Presidential commission investigating the causes of violence in America should begin work immediately after Robert F. Kennedy's funeral.

Higginbotham was one of two Negroes named to the commission by President Johnson. The other is Mrs. Patricia Harris, former U.S. Ambassador to Luxembourg.

Higginbotham, a friend of the Senator, joined the federal bench here in 1964 under an appointment made by President John F. Kennedy before he was assassinated.

"While we are all distraught over Senator Kennedy's death and the similar tragedies which have fallen on this nation by broad-scale violence and lawlessness as executed against public and nonpublic figures, it is essential that we as a nation not assume a posture of hopelessness," Higginbotham said, adding:

"I am convinced that our nation has the inherent capacity to come up with meaningful action programs which will be effective in eradicating some of the root causes of lawlessness and violence."

In San Francisco, Eric Hoffer, the longshoreman-philosopher appointed to a Presidential commission to investigate violence in America, said Americans were not violent at all.

"Basically we are the most gentle, generous, law-abiding and cooperative people on earth," the blunt-talking Hoffer said. "We are not violent!"

Hoffer said he had spent his life with "people considered the most violent on earth—skid row bums, migrant workers, longshoremen"—but had never seen a fight.

"These people and Americans, generally, are gentle, and orderly and kind. We must not be hasty. To accuse America because an Arab from Jerusalem committed this crime is the most slanderous thing in the world. These glib confessions of guilt are wrong."

Hoffer, a strong admirer of President Johnson, specifically criticized Senator Eugene McCarthy for putting "all the blame on the American people" for the assassination of Senator Robert F. Kennedy, and said violence was not committed by the masses but by the intelligentsia.

"We know that most violence is committed by the young and the educated," he said. "Wasn't Hitler an intellectual, wasn't Trotsky? Their kind of violence is not committed by the masses, but by an educated elite.

"We don't know why, but this is what we must learn."

"How often have you seen your neighbors fight?" he asked. "How often have you seen a street fight after an auto accident? No. We are understanding and cooperative. We settle our differences through orderly processes."

In Paris, the assassination of Senator Robert F. Kennedy has upset North Vietnam's strategy at the Vietnam War talks, conference sources said.

The Hanoi regime had been banking heavily on the growing dissension in the American political arena this summer during the Presidential campaigning. The sources said the North Vietnamese now apparently fear Kennedy's murder will close the ranks of the U.S. home front.

Officially, the North Vietnamese negotiators at the Paris talks have maintained diplomatic reserve and declined any comment about Kennedy's assassination on the ground that it falls under the heading "internal affairs" of the United States.

But Hanoi's strategy was known to be bound up in the American Presidential campaign and election.

Flags around the world were lowered to half staff. America's critics blamed an atmosphere of hate in the United States and said it proved the violent nature of its society. Its friends were shocked and rushed to send condolences.

In West Berlin, about 2,000 German youths marched silently through downtown streets Thursday night to honor the slain American Senator. The youths marched from Wittenberg Square to the plaza in front of the Schoeneberg city hall named for John F. Kennedy after he was assassinated.

U.S. embassies around the world opened black books of condolence for the slain Senator's admirers to sign as a token of grief. Kings and presidents cabled sympathy to the Senator's widow and President Johnson.

The Soviet Union expressed its official reaction in an editorial in the newspaper *Pravda*, which said political assassination is "an integral part of the American way of life."

"Violence, whether in Vietnam, or in Negro ghettoes or in the Hotel Ambassador, is the same American violence," *Pravda* said.

But as the news of Kennedy's death flashed through Moscow, private Russian citizens telephoned American news agency offices to express their sadness—a personal sadness unembittered by official Kremlin dogma.

One Central Telegraph Office official murmured quietly, "It's a nightmare."

East Germany went even further than the Soviet Union and said, "The planned, systematic extermination of people . . . has long been one of the main methods of American domestic politics."

Poland and Cuba echoed the theme, claiming the death of Kennedy was only further proof of an evil conspiracy in the United States and linked the assassinations of President John F. Kennedy and Dr. Martin Luther King Jr. to it.

"He was an inconvenient man for those who plotted the murder of President Kennedy," the Polish newspaper *Sycie Warszawy* said. It added that when it looked like Robert Kennedy might win the Presidential nomination "the odds are that the decision was taken to get rid of him."

In Havana, a television commentator implied President Johnson was involved and said, "There are some groups (in the U.S.) that do not want any Kennedy in the presidency, and they may be found in Washington and the White House."

Other communist nations were more sympathetic. The Czechoslovakian foreign ministry issued a statement which said "The Kennedy assassination was a shocking human tragedy not only for the United States. We also are deeply shocked."

Pope Paul VI offered prayers for Kennedy and sent messages to President Johnson and Mrs. Ethel Kennedy and, in a rare gesture, personally signed both cables. In his message to the President, the Roman Catholic Pontiff said he was "asking God to console, guard and bless you, your family, the government and people of the United States."

Messages of condolence poured in from all over the world. Queen Elizabeth II of Britain sent a personal message to Mrs. Kennedy and Prime Minister Harold Wilson also sent condolences. President Charles De Gaulle cabled both Mrs. Kennedy and President Johnson to express his sorrow.

From India, Kenya, Japan, Jordan, Pakistan, Finland, Sweden, Ireland, Denmark, Belgium and West Germany outflowings of grief and sympathy were cabled by national leaders. At the United Nations, Secretary General Thant led a procession of diplomats to the U.S. mission to sign a condolence book.

LYING IN STATE

Friday, June 7, 1968

Standing lonely vigil, an honor guard prays near the casket in the pre-dawn hours before the crowds come.

They Came to Say Goodbye

The line of people stretched a mile long, but they waited patiently to pay their final respects to "Bobby."

by Louis Cassels

NEW YORK (UPI) . . . The people who touched Bobby Kennedy's hand in life reached out Friday to touch his casket in death.

By the hundreds of thousands they came—rich and poor, black and white, old and young, male and female, immigrant and native-born—a vast polyglot stream of humanity united by a common sorrow.

Undeterred by 90-degree heat that turned midtown Manhattan into a bake-oven, they waited in line for upwards of seven hours in order to spend five seconds filing past the bier in St. Patrick's Cathedral where Robert Kennedy lay in state.

The throng of people wanting to say goodbye to the 42-year-old Senator was so great that authorities had to abandon plans to cut off the procession at 10 p.m. They announced that the great Neo-Gothic Roman Catholic cathedral on Fifth Avenue would remain open all night.

It was the biggest outpouring of grief in the big city's history.

Kennedy's body, flown here from Los Angeles, had remained overnight in the majestic cathedral on Fifth Avenue, but the public was not allowed to enter until shortly after 5:30 a.m. Hundreds had waited throughout the night for St. Patrick's great bronze doors to swing open. When the doors finally opened, the procession past the bier quickly reached a rate of 100 persons a minute. By the end of the day, 151,000 persons had passed through the cathedral.

A random 10-second sample included a tall blond in a miniskirt, her face contorted with sorrow; a middle-aged Negro woman wearing a shawl

Day and night tens of thousands of mourners waited patiently in line for a moment's view of the casket.

over her head, sobbing hard, being supported by her husband; a red-faced policeman, cap under arm, who had just gone off duty after guarding the cathedral through the night; two swarthy young men from Spanish Harlem, wearing sideburns and pointed shoes; a clutch of parochial school children, shepherded by two anxious young nuns; a man in a sports shirt who snapped a camera shot as he went by.

By early afternoon, the line of people waiting to get in stretched from Fifth Avenue along 51st Street to Park Avenue, down Park on one side to about 45th Street, back up Park 12 abreast to 52nd Street, and across 52nd Street to Lexington Avenue, where it doubled back four blocks to 48th Street.

As the first mourners passed by the bier, the voice of a priest could be heard:

"Let us pray that God will bless Bobby Kennedy, that God will bless this nation. . . .

"Let us pray that God will give the Kennedy family courage to endure this trying time. . ."

It was the little guy's day to honor a man who was born to wealth but always had a tremendous feeling for the poor and oppressed. They came by plane, by train, by car, and subway. Once inside, they filed somberly, respectfully past the bier. Some made the sign of the cross or genuflected. But the most characteristic gesture was to stretch forth a hand and touch the lid of the closed casket.

There is an old Irish superstition that touching a casket keeps the devil from troubling the soul of the deceased. But many who patted, rubbed, caressed, or kissed Kennedy's casket were plainly not of Irish descent. For them it was purely a gesture of affection—the same affection that led crowds to stampede after him, trying to touch him during his short but explosive Presidential campaign.

The casket rested on a bier draped in purple, in the crossing of the cathedral, where the wide center aisle intersects the side transepts. Six candles in tall bronze holders flanked it. A single wreath of white lilies lay at the foot. At first the African mahogany coffin had no cover, but later in the afternoon an American flag was draped over it.

Throughout the day, an honor guard of six men stood vigil around the coffin. The guard was changed frequently, consisting sometimes of members of the armed forces and at other times of relatives, friends, political associates, and staff aides of the late Senator. Participating in the honor guard were Attorney General Ramsey Clark, General Maxwell Taylor, U.N. Ambassador Arthur J. Goldberg, Ambassador-at-large W. Averell Harriman, actor Sidney Poitier, TV personality Jack Paar, and two of the slain Senator's sons.

146

Focus of a nation. The line of mourners enters St. Patrick's Cathedral on New York's Fifth Avenue.

At various times during the day members of the Kennedy family came and went quietly, mournfully, attending one or another of the eight masses said for their dead kinsman.

The Senator's widow, Ethel, pregnant with their 11th child, came to the cathedral at noon with her three eldest children. They knelt in a front pew while a priest, offering a mass for the dead, intoned the prayer:

"May light eternal shine upon him, O Lord . . . be merciful to the soul of your faithful servant Robert."

Mrs. Kennedy, whose trademark is a hairbow, wore a black one for this sad occasion. Her eyes were wide and staring.

But mostly it was the people's day. And as it wore on, the blistering heat began to take its toll. The Red Cross said it treated 65 persons in the street for exhaustion. A Red Cross truck pulled up on 51st Street outside the cathedral and volunteers dispensed cups of water and orange- and grapefruit juice to mourners. In their eagerness to grasp the refreshments, some persons reached over the barricades, threatening to overturn them.

"I've been waiting for more than six hours," said a perspiring, heavy-set woman. "This is the first drink I've had."

Later, vendors arrived, selling orange juice in small containers for between 25 and 40 cents.

While they waited in line outside the cathedral, the people talked and laughed among themselves. At one point a group of Negroes and whites broke into strains of the civil rights anthem "We Shall Overcome," changing the chorus to "no more violence," and "no more selling guns."

As the line neared St. Patrick's, it picked up speed. Inside the door, a policeman shattered the quiet with the repeated call: "Single file. Keep in a single file."

Some of the mourners entered pews and knelt in prayer. Others just walked slowly by the casket and out a side door. Many of the faces were streaked with tears as they left the cathedral, but there were only a few outbursts of emotion.

One woman with a German accent began screaming, "No! No!" as she neared the casket. When patrolmen escorted her to a side door, she shouted: "Don't take me away. I want to see him."

Another woman whose cries reverberated through the cathedral had to be helped to a pew and given smelling salts. "Let me stay here, let me stay here," she cried. Then as she quieted down, she sobbed softly, "Why, why?"

That was the question that troubled them all.

"I Hadta Come to This Thing"

Few could say exactly why they stood on the long, agonizing line outside the cathedral. They just "hadta."

by Milton R. Benjamin

NEW YORK (UPI) . . . The wind-up alarm clock went off at 6:15 in Joe Gagliardi's room in a Garfield, N.J., boardinghouse. He pulled on a pair of slacks and walked down the hall to the pay phone to call his boss at the tire factory.

"I won't be in to run the machine today," he told him. "I think I've got the flu." Then Joe went back to his room, pulled on a pink sport shirt, and caught the bus to New York and St. Patrick's Cathedral. Thousands of others had the same idea.

"The highway was just jammed with buses," Joe said. "It looked like everybody in the whole country was coming to pay their respects. It's a terrible thing. He was the only guy that coulda brought the whites and Negroes and everybody together."

Outside the majestic cathedral in midtown Manhattan, tens of thousands of whites, Negroes and Puerto Ricans stood sweating, shoulder-to-shoulder, in a line that snaked through city streets for more than a mile.

"I hadta come to this thing," Joe said. He had been standing in the line in the 90-degree heat for more than two hours. The pink shirt was unbuttoned, his T shirt was soaked through, and the front of the line was still about 12 blocks away.

"Even if I don't get inta see him, it's important to me justa be here,"

149

he said. A computer programmer, whose thermos bottle of iced tea had run out a half-hour earlier, nodded in agreement.

"And I'll tell you this," he said, jabbing a finger toward Joe. "Just between you and me, buddy, I'd sure like to be alone in that cell with that guy for just five minutes." Persons within earshot muttered their approval.

Mourner faints during long wait to enter the Cathedral. Heat hit over 90°.

While a woman kneels to touch the coffin, Robert Jr. and TV personality Jack Paar stand as guards of honor.

Private Grief, Public Strength

Each in his own way, the Kennedys paid homage to the fallen Senator, but always with stoic dignity and restraint.

NEW YORK (UPI) . . . Mrs. Joseph P. Kennedy arrived at St. Patrick's Cathedral early Friday morning. Dressed in black, heavily veiled, she took her daily communion at a side altar. She shared her prayer book with a soldier who sat next to her. The soldier, José Indart of New York, said he recognized her but pretended he had not.

She did not approach her son's bier and few aside from Indart knew she was there.

Few knew either that the weeping woman helped through a side door and into a waiting car by two uniformed policemen 80 minutes later was Rose Kennedy.

Mrs. Kennedy had not cried in public before, but this was the third son she had lost. Her husband, paralyzed by a stroke in 1961, had remained behind in Hyannis Port, Mass., where he received holy communion.

Senator Edward Kennedy, the last surviving son, had come to St. Patrick's earlier, sitting alone during a 6 a.m. mass. The 36-year-old Senator had spent almost the entire night in the cathedral, maintaining a lonely vigil over his brother's coffin.

Ethel Kennedy, black dress, black bow in her short hair, went to the cathedral at midday. She moved before the thousands in the vaulted chamber, before the television cameras, as though in a trance. Her eyes were wide and the pain of her new widowhood showed on her face.

Her three oldest children, Kathleen, 16; Joseph III, 15; and Robert Jr., 14; her sisters-in-law, Eunice Shriver and Patricia Lawford, and others were with her.

Mrs. John F. Kennedy prays for her slain brother-in-law.

A widow's grief at the noon mass for the dead.

Both the great and the humble filed past the casket in silent tribute. Above, Mrs. Martin Luther King Jr., widow of another assassinated leader.

Top, leader of the poor peoples' march Rev. Ralph Abernathy accompanies Mrs. John F. Kennedy and her sister, Princess Lee Radziwill. Below left, Pierre Salinger, press secretary of President John F. Kennedy.

They passed the bier, where each son had served his turn in the honor guard earlier in the morning. They prayed.

Jacqueline Kennedy followed. Except for the Secret Service escort she has had since her husband too was assassinated, she was alone. Again the cameras and the crowds watched as she prayed behind white-gloved hands, paused to touch the coffin, to cross herself, and left.

This was the public mourning. But they also mourned in private. And everyone close to them was fierce in determination to preserve what privacy there was. "The last thing we want to do is to follow them around today," one aide to the late Senator said.

Jacqueline Kennedy and another Kennedy sister, Jean Smith, had their Fifth Avenue apartments in which to retire. For Ethel Kennedy there was the apartment in a modern United Nations Plaza skyscraper overlooking the East River. Rose Kennedy had her New York pied-à-terre on Central Park South.

Edward Kennedy and his wife, Joan, stayed at the Carlyle Hotel, small and elegant, in the East 70s, which became the New York White House when John F. Kennedy was President. Eunice and Sargent Shriver, the new Ambassador to France, also stayed there along with Jacqueline Kennedy's sister, Princess Lee Radziwill, and her husband, Stanislas.

"They have been exceedingly quiet today, but of course they came in quite late last night," a hotel spokesman said Friday afternoon. "They are generally staying close to the hotel and visiting among themselves."

Jacqueline Kennedy was waiting for the arrival of her stepfather and mother, Mr. and Mrs. Hugh D. Auchincloss from their Newport, R.I., estate, Hammersmith Farm. They flew to New York in late afternoon, bringing with them young Caroline and John Kennedy.

With her mother, her children, and a playmate of Caroline's, young Mary Nelson, Mrs. Kennedy returned to the cathedral late Friday. "There's Jackie Kennedy. Jackie Kennedy's here," came the cry from the crowd as they arrived.

Ethel Kennedy also returned to the church at 8:30 p.m., led to the bier by singer Andy Williams, a personal friend of the family. Walking behind Mrs. Kennedy was pro football player Roosevelt Grier, who had helped seize the accused gunman.

Minutes before Mrs. Kennedy arrived, Williams sang "Ave Maria" at a brief service conducted by Archbishop Terence J. Cooke.

Mrs. Kennedy and a daughter broke down and wept as they sat near the catafalque. It was the sight of the girl in tears that broke Mrs. Kennedy's reserve. The two embraced and consoled each other.

And the Tributes Go On

*Condolences continue to pour in from the
great and the small throughout the world.*

A peasant woman knelt by flickering candles in a Warsaw church and prayed for the soul of Robert F. Kennedy. Pope Paul VI offered mass in his private chapel in Vatican City. United Nations delegations of 124 countries stood in silence for one minute.

Millions around the world mourned the death of the brother of a murdered American President in gestures ranging from special services and public tributes to individual condolences and visits to U.S. embassies.

A Calcutta newspaper summed up India's reaction to the assassination of the New York Senator in a front-page cartoon: It shows Columbus in a boat covering both of his eyes and saying, "I wish I had not discovered America."

While many Russians privately expressed their shock and grief, the official Soviet press speculated that both the Senator and his brother, President John F. Kennedy, were victims of right-wing plots.

The government newspaper *Izvestia* seized on the report of the search for the woman who allegedly shouted, "We shot him," to bolster the conspiracy theory. The Soviet communist party's newspaper *Pravda* wrote of "capitalist America which is symbolized by murders in Vietnam, Mississippi, Texas, Tennessee and California."

A black leather book of condolences was opened for one day at the U.S. Embassy in Moscow but only two middle-level Soviet Foreign Ministry officials were sent to sign it.

A similar book in the U.S. Embassy in Warsaw was filled with hundreds of signatures of Poles who waited in line to enter the embassy to register their condolences and leave flowers by a Kennedy portrait.

Stefan Cardinal Wyszynski, the Polish Primate, will hold a requiem mass for Kennedy on Monday.

Flags lowered to half-staff before the nation's Capitol.

The Japanese government awarded the nation's highest decoration to the Senator. The First Class Order of the Grand Cordon of the Rising Sun was awarded posthumously "in appreciation of his efforts for the promotion of Japanese-American friendship."

Memorial services for Kennedy were scheduled in Japan, Thailand, Malaysia and scores of other countries.

Radio Hanoi said the assassination revealed the "ugly face of the rotten capitalistic society in America."

"The assassinations of the Kennedy brothers are proof of deepening conflicts among the American capitalists," the radio said.

North Vietnam's official daily *Nhan Dan* said, "This doubtless was a political assassination which was closely connected with the life and death race for the U.S. Presidency."

The semi-official Cairo newspaper *Al Ahram* said, "We can only regret" Kennedy's death.

"The true killer of Robert Kennedy is . . . a mixture of violence which characterizes American life and prejudice against the cause of people who want to live," *Al Ahram* said in an editorial.

It said that Sirhan Bishara Sirhan, the 24-year-old Arab immigrant accused of murdering the Senator, "is a natural product of the atmosphere of violence in America."

Sirhan has spent the last 11 years in the United States, "and these were decisive years in his mental and psychological growth," the paper said.

In Berlin, 2,000 young West Germans marched silently through downtown streets to John F. Kennedy Square for a ceremony at a monument erected in honor of the late President, the Senator's brother.

In Stockholm, the assassination cast a shadow over traditional National Day celebrations and speakers at patriotic gatherings eulogized him.

Acting Prime Minister John McEwen of Australia ordered all flags in Canberra at half-staff and expressed the "deep feeling of sympathy in the hearts of the Australian people."

The Portuguese Foreign Minister, Alberto Franco Nogueira, sent a cablegram expressing his sorrow and said, "Such a violent crime deserves the condemnation of all men."

Flags in Jamaica flew at half-staff and Prime Minister Hugh Shearer said he expected to be in Washington for the funeral.

In Paris, newsmen on strike at the state-owned broadcasting networks sent a message that said they regretted not being able to inform the French public of "these critical times in the history of the United States."

President Juan Carlos Ongania of Argentina went on television to deplore violence in the United States and to "thank God peace reigns in our country."

161

From Seoul, President Chung Hee Park of South Korea sent a message to Kennedy's widow saying the Korean people were "shocked to learn of the tragic death."

But 700 million persons remained ignorant of Kennedy's death in Communist China, where the official propaganda outlets made no mention of it.

Pope offers private mass

VATICAN CITY (UPI) . . . Pope Paul VI offered mass today for the repose of the soul of Senator Robert F. Kennedy.

Vatican sources said the Roman Catholic Pontiff celebrated the mass in his private chapel adjoining his apartment in the Apostolic Palace.

Only the Pope's two private secretaries were present at the service, the sources said.

The Pope prayed for Kennedy and his family throughout Wednesday and Thursday. He celebrated mass for the Senator, imploring "the mercy of the Lord," several hours before Kennedy died.

Vatican spokesman Msgr. Fausto Vallainc said the Pope learned of the death with "mournful sadness," and went immediately to the chapel to pray for him.

Later the Pope personally dictated messages of "sincere condolences" to President Lyndon B. Johnson and the Senator's widow.

Pope Paul personally signed the cables, showing his deep concern over the assassination. Amleto Cardinal Cicognani, the Vatican Secretary of State, normally signs such messages in the Pope's name.

The Pope dispatched one of his top aides, Angelo Cardinal Dell'Acqua, Papal Vicar for Rome, to New York to act as his personal representative at the funeral and convey a special papal benediction.

Sirhan Indicted

First degree murder indictment against accused assassin Sirhan Bishara Sirhan comes after a daylong hearing.

by Myram Borders

LOS ANGELES (UPI) . . . Swarthy Sirhan Bishara Sirhan was indicted today for the assassination of Senator Robert F. Kennedy and later arraigned under super-security precautions in a jail chapel.

If convicted, the 24-year-old native of Jordan could be executed in the state gas chamber.

The first degree murder indictment was voted by the Los Angeles County Grand Jury after a daylong hearing. Sirhan also was indicted on five counts of assault with intent to commit murder.

(Six days after the hearing, testimony of witnesses before the grand jury was released, revealing that a third bullet had also struck Kennedy below the armpit and that Sirhan had been seen in conversation with the mysterious "woman in the polka dot dress" immediately before the shooting.)

For Sirhan, the arraignment was his first public appearance since enraged Kennedy party members and hotel workers seized him in a wild melee as the Senator slumped to the floor with bullets in his head and shoulder.

Sirhan was brought into the third floor chapel of the jail for his arraignment. The 24-year-old Jordanian immigrant sat at the foot of a marble-topped altar that served as the judge's bench and heard the grand jury indictment charging him with the murder "of Robert Francis Kennedy, a human being."

Only newsmen who had been carefully identified and searched were allowed into the chapel by sheriff's deputies determined to protect Sirhan from the fate of Lee Harvey Oswald, who was shot down in a Dallas police garage two days after the assassination of President John F. Kennedy.

No one other than court officials, law officers, and newsmen was permitted to attend the arraignment. Security was so tight that many officers, including a police captain, had to surrender their pistols.

Sirhan, a tiny figure with a thick bush of black curly hair, was brought into the makeshift courtroom on the third floor of the maximum security men's county jail in a wheelchair through a door facing the spectators.

As 200 newsmen and officers crowded into the chapel, for the half-hour proceeding, the defendant, dressed in a short-sleeved white shirt open at the neck and blue jail jeans, was wheeled to the foot of the altar steps where he stood up and climbed the two steps to his chair. His left index finger, which was broken during the struggle at his capture, was in a splint and his left ankle, which was sprained, was heavily bandaged.

After telling the court he couldn't afford an attorney, he was formally assigned the Public Defender to handle his case. Sirhan's next court proceeding was set for June 28 at 9 a.m. when he will be asked to enter a plea to the indictment.

Sirhan's chair was placed so that his back was to the crowd. Massed behind him were four burly sheriff's deputies to make it impossible for anyone to shoot or attack him.

When he was wheeled into the room, Sirhan looked curiously at the newsmen. He tapped a foot during the proceedings but showed little emotion or concern for his ankle and left index finger.

As he came down the steps afterwards, Sirhan grimaced or smiled. Newsmen were unable to agree as to his exact expression.

Eighteen deputies were in the chapel, including one who paced along a balcony that ran along the back of the chapel.

When Superior Court Judge Arthur L. Alarcon read his name, Sirhan corrected the pronunciation. Alarcon called him "Sir-hahn" and the defendant said he was "Sir-han."

When asked if he had money for counsel, Sirhan replied, "No, sir."

The lengthy indictment was read count by count by Deputy District Attorney John Howard. Then the jurist appointed two psychiatrists to examine Sirhan at the request of the Public Defender.

When a representative of the American Civil Liberties Union said

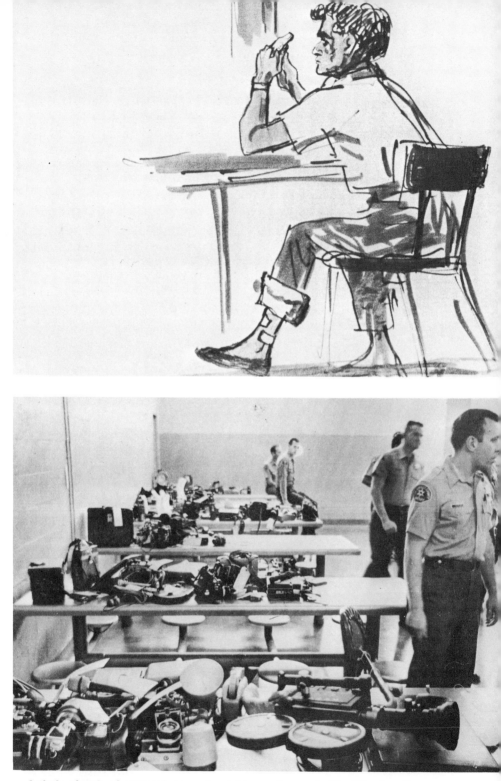

Artist's sketch of accused assassin at his arraignment. Sheriff's deputies removed all cameras from newsmen attending the hearing.

Sirhan wanted to be represented by counsel other than the Public Defender, the judge said this was not the proper time to consider the request.

Alarcon presided from the marble-topped altar flanked by a United States flag on the left and a California flag on the right. Two hooks were visible on the wall behind the altar where the cross had been taken down.

In the opening proceedings Alarcon intoned:

"Department 100 of Superior Court is now in session. The record will show that Department 100 of Superior Court is sitting at this time in temporary courtroom provided by the sheriff because of the defendant's present physical condition and to avoid the possibility that any incident might occur that would deny the defendant the right to a fair trial."

When Sirhan was asked by the jurist if the arrangements were agreeable to him, he replied in a firm voice, "Yes, sir."

The psychiatrists named by Alarcon were Drs. Eric Marcus and Edward Steinbook. The jurist emphasized the appointment could not be construed to mean the court had any contention as to Sirhan's sanity and was acting only at the request of the defense.

As Sirhan left the chapel to return to the hospital section of the jail in another wing on the second floor, the judge ordered everyone to remain in the pews.

In other developments in another hectic day for Los Angeles authorities:

—Police disclosed Sirhan's shabby, old-model car was located near the Ambassador Hotel, scene of the assassination. The 1956 pink and white DeSoto was checked for fingerprints and impounded.

—Hundreds of "tips" that others were involved in the shooting were received and checked. Police discounted all theories on a possible conspiracy.

—A Kennedy campaign worker surrendered as the mystery woman in the polka dot dress seen fleeing from the hotel screaming, "We shot him." She was released after convincing officers it was all a misunderstanding.

She was Kathy Fulmer, 19, a Los Angeles brunette who said she was wearing a green suit with a polka dot scarf at the Kennedy victory celebration. After witnessing the shooting, she said, she ran from the hotel yelling, "He's been shot."

Another campaign worker had triggered the nationwide alert by reporting she saw a woman in a polka dot dress race from the hotel screaming, "We shot him."

Thousands walked by Kennedy's casket in New York City as the 22-member grand jury—14 women and 8 men—acted in Los Angeles' Hall of Justice. Earlier jurors heard testimony from 22 witnesses in a 6 hour session followed by 25 minutes of deliberation.

Although the jury proceedings were closed, it was known the testimony touched on the rapidity of the shooting, ensuing bedlam, efforts to save Kennedy's life during a speeding ambulance ride, a complex brain operation, and target practice by Sirhan hours before the assassination.

The dramatic report of Sirhan's target practice with a .22 caliber pistol came from Henry Carreon, who talked to the defendant Tuesday at a Southern California mountain shooting range.

Carreon had told police he noticed Sirhan because of his rapid firing, which was not permitted on the range. He said they then talked briefly about the pistol.

Three hotel workers who helped subdue Sirhan were among those called before the jury, as was a department inspector who took a photograph of the struggle moments after the shooting.

Former Olympic decathlon champion Rafer Johnson and professional football star Roosevelt Grier—credited with major roles in Sirhan's capture—were excused from testifying because they were in New York for final rites for the Senator.

Two of the five persons injured in the burst of gunfire that felled the Senator in a kitchen corridor of the Ambassador Hotel early Wednesday were among the witnesses before the jury. Both declined to comment on their testimony under instructions from the District Attorney's office.

They were Irwin Stroll, 17, who was brought to the hearing on a chaise lounge-like device, and Ira Goldstein, 19, a radio newsman. Both suffered leg wounds, but Goldstein was released from a hospital Thursday and was capable of walking without assistance.

When asked for his reaction to the announcement of Kennedy's death 25½ hours after the shooting, Goldstein said:

"I kind of cried a little bit. Then, I forced myself to walk for the first time."

Goldstein said he did not see the assassin as he walked behind Kennedy. When asked where he was as Kennedy was shot, Goldstein replied: "I was where he was a few seconds before . . ."

As newsmen swarmed around Stroll in the Hall of Justice, an archaic architectural achievement of jumbled rooms and corridors, the youngster kept repeating, "Watch out for my leg."

Peering intensely through horn-rimmed glasses, Stroll said the leg wound hurt "off and on" but he was not under sedation. His legs were covered with a sheet.

The first witness before the jury was silver-haired Paul Ziffren, former California Democratic National Committeeman. He was called presumably to identify the victim as being Kennedy.

Ziffren was followed by Dr. Henry Cuneo, one of the six neurosurgeons who battled to save the Senator's life in a pre-dawn brain operation. Cuneo also participated in an autopsy before Kennedy's body was taken to New York to lie in state at St. Patrick's Cathedral.

Other witnesses included Coroner Thomas Noguchi, a police officer who was first to reach the scene, and several hotel employes.

Dishwasher Jesus Perez gave newsmen a preview of his testimony before being whisked into the witnesses' room adjoining the paneled, high-ceiling jury chamber. Perez was shaking Kennedy's hand when eight shots rang out.

A slight, bespectacled young man, Perez said at first he thought the shots were noises made by someone trying to clear the path for the Senator. Perez said Kennedy's hand slipped from his grasp and he toppled to the concrete floor.

The dishwasher said Sirhan had waited in the kitchen area for about 30 minutes and asked three or four times if Kennedy would pass through the narrow passageway leading to the freight elevator.

Asked if Sirhan seemed nervous or whether anyone was with him, Perez replied:

"He looked worried—not nervous. I didn't see anyone with him."

Another witness who gave newsmen a preview of his testimony was ambulance attendant Richard Walker. He treated television newsman William Weisel, who was among the wounded in the shooting.

Walker quoted Weisel as saying he "was standing three steps behind the Senator and, all of a sudden, felt three sharp stings in his side, and saw the Senator fall after he had already been shot. He had a real funny look on his face."

The jury foreman was balding L. E. McKee, 65, a retired garage chain owner.

The jury, composed of 14 women and 8 men, normally totals 23, but one member was on vacation. A vote of 14 is needed for an indictment.

The first witness appeared before the jury at 9:30 a.m. and the final one at 3:55 p.m. Accompanied by four helmeted sheriff's deputies, McKee left the fifth floor jury chambers at 4:30 p.m. to return the indictment to Superior Court Department 100 on the eighth floor.

The witnesses

LOS ANGELES (UPI) . . . Twenty-two witnesses, ranging from a bus boy to a former Democratic National Committeeman, reconstructed the shooting of Senator Robert F. Kennedy for the grand jury Friday.

168

The witnesses, and their reported connection with the case, were:

1. Paul Ziffren, former Democratic National Committeeman from California. He was called to identify Kennedy as the man who was killed.

2. Dr. Henry Cuneo, a neurosurgeon who participated in the brain operation attempting to save Kennedy's life.

3. Dr. Thomas T. Noguchi, chief medical examiner, county coroner, and a pathologist who directed the autopsy performed on Kennedy's body.

4. Sgt. Albert J. Lavalle, Los Angeles Police Department cartographer who made drawings of the murder scene.

5. Irwin Stroll, 17, wounded in the gunfire at the Ambassador Hotel where Kennedy was killed.

6. Travis R. White, one of the two police officers who took Sirhan into custody.

7. Jesus Perez, hotel dishwasher who was shaking hands with Kennedy when he was shot.

8. Vincent Di Pierro, hotel banquet employee who reportedly helped subdue Sirhan.

9. Ira Goldstein, a broadcasting company employee who was wounded by one of the bullets.

10. Arthur Placencia, the second police officer who took Sirhan into custody.

11. Karl Uecker, Assistant Banquet Manager at the hotel. He also reportedly helped detain Sirhan.

12. Eddie Minasisan, another hotel employee who reportedly aided in subduing Sirhan.

13. Harold Burba, a Los Angeles City fire department inspector who took a photograph of Sirhan struggling with two men immediately after the shooting.

14. Henry Carreon, reported to have seen Sirhan at a San Gabriel target shooting range hours before the assassination, and to have briefly talked to him about his rapid firing of a .22 caliber, nine-shot pistol.

15. Dr. V. Faustin Bazilauskas, a doctor who treated the wounded at Central Receiving Hospital.

16. Robert Hulsman, an ambulance driver for Central Receiving Hospital.

17. Max Behrman, Hulsman's assistant.

18. Jerrold Hemmingway, driver for a private ambulance company.

19. Donald Rus, a Central Receiving Hospital ambulance driver.

20. Lt. Charles Hughes, commander of the police department's Rampart Division Detective Squad.

21. Lt. Al Hegge, a detective from the Rampart Division.

22. De Wayne Wolfer, police ballistics expert.

Super-Security at arraignment

Newsmen attending the arraignment of Sirhan were carefully screened before being allowed to enter the jail chapel.

"We were taken to a third floor dining hall, where we were thoroughly searched—the women more closely than the men," reported UPI staffer Joan Sweeney. "I was taken into a small pantry where a matron went through my hair, looked in my mouth, searched my clothes, my shoes and even looked at the soles of my feet. My purse and my coat were taken away from me and I was allowed only a notepad and a pen after a careful check of the latter.

"After the search was completed we were given another pass which allowed us to enter the chapel. No one could leave until the arraignment was over and the defendant was taken away."

"It is like talking to someone on the Moon"

by Tracy Wood

LOS ANGELES (UPI) . . . Trying to carry on a conversation with accused assassin Sirhan Sirhan "is like talking to someone on the moon," according to District Attorney Evelle Younger.

Younger, a former FBI agent, said all conversation between his assistants and Sirhan had been one-sided. Younger himself had not talked to Sirhan.

Extensive security measures were underway at the Los Angeles County Jail as a result of telephoned threats against Sirhan, but Younger expressed concern for future court proceedings.

"There are some people in the world who will want to make our country and our system of justice look bad," he said. "Anything that is said in connection with this case will be scrutinized by politicians all over the world.

"If someone steps on his (Sirhan's) toe it will be headlines all over the world."

The dark-haired district attorney chatted with newsmen in a hallway near the Grand Jury Room in the Hall of Justice.

Younger made it clear he planned to avoid any incidents such as happened in the aftermath of the assassination of President John F. Kennedy in Dallas in 1963. Accused assassin Lee Harvey Oswald was gunned down by gambler Jack Ruby, who later died of cancer.

"If he couldn't get a fair trial in Los Angeles," Younger said of Sirhan, "he obviously couldn't get it in Hayes City, Kan. I definitely think he can get a fair trial and will get a fair trial here."

The girl in the polka dot dress

LOS ANGELES (UPI) . . . A pretty 19-year-old brunette surrendered to sheriff's deputies here saying she believed she was the mysterious woman in a polka dot dress wanted for questioning in connection with the assassination of Senator Robert F. Kennedy.

Kathy Fulmer called the sheriff's department and two deputies were dispatched to nearby Chinatown to pick her up.

After questioning by deputies the teen-ager was transferred to police headquarters where an informal bulletin had been issued seeking information on her whereabouts for interrogation. Less than three hours later she was released.

"She's been taken home, there's no hold on her," a desk officer said.

Miss Fulmer told newsmen she was standing close to Sirhan shortly before the fatal shots were fired. She said she "was one of the first people to know Senator Kennedy was shot." Her grief-stricken cries, "He's been shot!" were misunderstood, she said.

Deputies said Miss Fulmer contacted the sheriff's office "because I didn't want to go to the police station."

Deputies said Miss Fulmer called Captain Lisle Fields of the sheriff's information bureau and identified herself as "Sunday Rossi, 19." They said the girl told Captains Fields she thought she was wanted in the shooting and was in nearby Chinatown.

Two men picked the girl up and took her to the Hall of Justice where she was interviewed.

After she had talked with newsmen for a few moments, the sheriff advised her to make no further statements. She told newsmen she had recently moved to Los Angeles and could not remember her exact address.

FUNERAL
and
BURIAL

Saturday, June 8, 1968

A private moment after the great bronze doors of the Cathedral closed to the public about 5 a.m. on Saturday.

Richard Cardinal Cushing of Boston blesses the coffin with holy water toward end of the solemn requiem mass.

The Last Mass

*The world watches on TV as elaborate service
is conducted at St. Patrick's Cathedral.*

by Louis Cassels

NEW YORK (UPI) . . . A sorrowing nation and a family still stunned by the unbelievability of its loss Saturday commended to God the soul of Robert F. Kennedy, "a good and decent man" whose life of service to others was cut off at the age of 42 by a bullet from an assassin's gun.

The last mass to be said over Kennedy—a faithful Catholic who attended mass almost every day of his adult life—was celebrated in St. Patrick's Cathedral in the presence of 6 cardinals, including a personal emissary of Pope Paul VI; 6 archbishops; 18 bishops and more than 200 priests.

Among the 2,300 invited guests were President and Mrs. Johnson and four men who were Kennedy's rivals in the 1968 Presidential campaign— Vice President Hubert H. Humphrey, Senator Eugene McCarthy, former Vice President Richard M. Nixon, and Governor Nelson A. Rockefeller. TV coverage of the ceremonies was broadcast to other parts of the world by space satellite.

Chief Justice Earl Warren; Secretary of State Dean Rusk and other members of the Cabinet; leaders of Congress and the armed forces; the "beautiful people" of the smart Kennedy set in Washington, New York and Newport; and humble people whose lives somehow got involved with the many-faceted career of Bobby Kennedy also were in the solemn-faced crowd which filled every seat of the 450-foot long Neo-Gothic church on Fifth Avenue.

At the conclusion of the hour and 45 minute service, Kennedy's flag-draped mahogany casket began its final journey by train to Washington for burial in Arlington National Cemetery.

The funeral service climaxed 40 hours of mourning for New York,

177

"... a good and decent man." Senator Edward Kennedy eulogizes his brother. Listeners include, from right to left, President Lyndon Johnson, a Secret Service man, Chief Justice Earl Warren, and—far left—New York City Mayor John Lindsay.

Sons and daughters, nieces and nephews of Robert Kennedy return from the altar after delivering offerings for the mass.

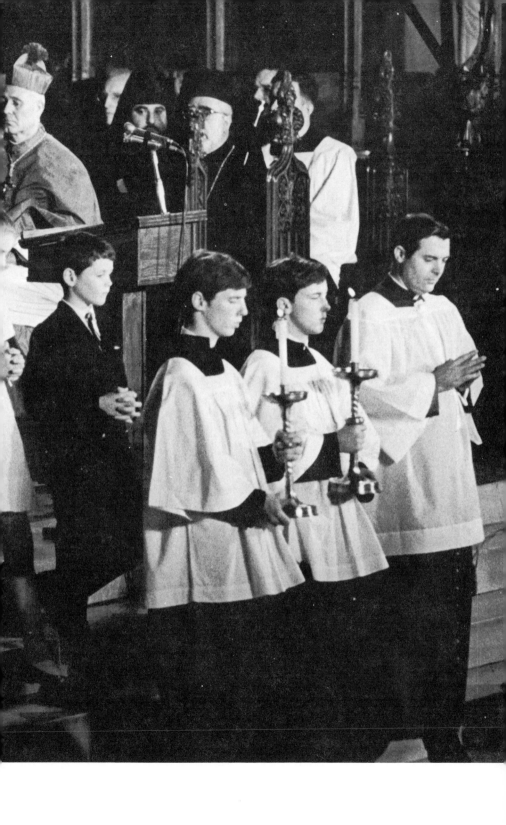

Young Robert Jr. wipes a tear from his eye as he sits next to his cousin Christopher Lawford.

Kennedy's adopted city. His grip on the affections of the "little people" whose cause he espoused was plainly demonstrated by the willingness of 151,000 of them to stand in line for as long as six hours in order to spend a few seconds filing past his casket as it lay in state at St. Patrick's Friday and all through Friday night.

The Kennedy family, caught up in the incredible nightmare of repeating an experience that seemed too horrible to be endured twice, filled nearly a dozen front rows of the cathedral.

Senator Edward M. Kennedy—young Ted, once the baby of the family, now the only survivor of four distinguished brothers—spoke for all the Kennedys in a brief personal message before the mass got underway.

His face a stolid mask of controlled agony, his voice occasionally breaking with emotion, he described his brother Bobby as "a good and decent man" who "saw wrong and tried to right it, saw suffering and tried to heal it, saw war and tried to stop it."

On behalf of the whole family—from his often-bereaved 77-year-old mother Rose, to the widow and 10 fatherless children of Robert Kennedy —the young Senator said with simple eloquence:

"We loved him . . . he gave us strength in time of trouble, wisdom in time of uncertainty . . .

"Those of us who loved him . . . pray that what he wished for others will some day come to pass for all the world."

Richard Cardinal Cushing, the intrepid old man of God who has been a sort of pastor-extraordinary to the Kennedy family, presided over the mass and conducted the final ceremony of blessing the body by anointing the casket with holy water and perfuming it with incense.

In the gravel-voiced Irish accent which the nation remembers from John F. Kennedy's inauguration and funeral, the 72-year-old Archbishop of Boston intoned the ancient prayer for the soul of a dead Christian:

"May the angels take you into paradise; may the martyrs come to welcome you on your way, and lead you into the Holy City . . . may the choir of angels welcome you and with Lazarus who was once poor may you have everlasting rest."

Archbishop Terence Cooke of New York delivered a 20-minute eulogy from St. Patrick's high marble pulpit. He said Robert Kennedy was "a man of faith—faith in God first of all, but faith also in the basic goodness of his fellow man and faith in the future of his country."

Looking down at President Johnson, who sat with a somber expression in the first row on the left side of the church, Archbishop Cooke commended the President for telling the nation in a television talk Wednesday that "200 million Americans did not fire the shot that ended Senator Kennedy's life."

The face of grief.

"The act of one man must not demoralize and incapacitate 200 million others," the Archbishop said. "To permit this would be to fail utterly to grasp the message of hope and optimism in Senator Kennedy's life."

Ethel Kennedy, the Senator's widow, who is pregnant with their 11th child, entered the cathedral just before the service began, on the arm of her brother-in-law Ted. She sat in the front pew on the right side of the church, with Ted on her left, next to the aisle. On her right in the same pew were four of her five oldest children: Kathleen, 16; Joseph P. III, 15; David, 12; and Mary Courtney, 11. The second oldest son, Robert Jr., 14, served as an altar boy.

Also in the front family pew with Ethel was Jacqueline Kennedy, widowed in the same way, and from the stricken look of her face, painfully reliving the whole nightmare of 1963; and her two children, Caroline, 11, and John Jr., 7.

After the sermon, when the service was more than halfway over, the five younger children of Robert Kennedy were brought into the cathedral through a private side entrance to sit with their mother. The baby, 14-month-old Douglas Harriman Kennedy, stayed only a moment to look with bewildered eyes at his father's casket, then was taken out of the church by a nurse.

Ethel Kennedy stared straight ahead, her face a hollow-eyed mask of suffering, throughout the service. She managed not to weep, even when she went forward on Ted's arm to receive communion. But at times during the long prayers, she seemed to nestle behind her brother-in-law's broad shoulders, as though trying to hide from all the eyes watching to see how she would bear up under this ordeal.

John F. Kennedy Jr., already a speaking likeness of his father, provided one of the most poignant moments of the long ceremony when he offered his arm to escort his 77-year-old grandmother, Mrs. Rose Kennedy, to the communion rail.

At the end of the service, entertainer Andy Williams brought tears and sobs to many when he sang the familiar words:

"As he died to make men holy, let us die to make men free."

Archbishop Cooke: "Our sense of shame and discouragement tears alone will not wash away."

NEW YORK (UPI) . . . Archbishop Terence J. Cooke, delivering a eulogy at the funeral of slain Senator Robert F. Kennedy, warned Americans

Senator Eugene McCarthy walks past the flag-draped coffin after receiving Holy Communion.

ROBERT FRANCIS KENNEDY
November 20, 1925 – June 6, 1968

†

Dear God,
Please take care of him who tried to take care of yours.

❧   ❧   ❧

"Come, my friends,
Tis not too late to seek a newer world"
                                    —Tennyson, Ulysses

"Aeschylus wrote: 'In our sleep, pain that cannot forget
falls drop by drop upon the heart and in our own despair,
against our will, comes wisdom through the awful grace
of God.'

"What we need in the United States . . . is love and
wisdom and compassion toward one another, and a feeling of justice toward those who still suffer within our
own country, whether they be white or they be black.

"Let us dedicate ourselves to what the Greeks wrote so
many years ago: to tame the savageness of man and
make gentle the life of the world. Let us dedicate ourselves to that, and say a prayer for our country and for
our people."

                                    —Robert F. Kennedy
                                    *Extemporaneous remarks on the death of
                                    Martin Luther King, Indianapolis, Indiana
                                    April 4, 1968*

**Police carefully searched persons attending the funeral. The security check
turned up an unloaded pistol in one briefcase. All those attending received this
remembrance card.**

watching the services throughout the country against letting the act of one man "demoralize and incapacitate 200 million others."

"To permit this to happen would be to fail utterly to grasp the message of hope and optimism in Senator Kennedy's life," the Roman Catholic Archbishop of New York declared.

"We salute the sense of purpose which gave direction to Robert Kennedy's life," the Archbishop said. That purpose, he said, was "to build a better world for all his fellow men."

The Archbishop quoted President Johnson's "wise counsel when he pointed out that 200 million Americans did not fire the shot that ended Senator Kennedy's life."

"Our sense of shame and discouragement tears alone will not wash away," he said. "Somehow, by the grace of God, and with the strength that still lies deep within the soul of America, we must find the courage to take up again the laborious work to which Senator Kennedy devoted all his energies: the building of a great and honorable nation."

World Leaders Attend Funeral

NEW YORK (UPI) . . . Prime ministers, a vice president, a prince of the church, and ambassadors attended the funeral mass, including:
Ireland—Prime Minister John Lynch.
Jamaica—Prime Minister Hugh Shearer.
Guyana—Prime Minister Forbes Burnham.
The Vatican—Angelo Cardinal Dell'Acqua, Papal Vicar of Rome and close friend of the Kennedy family.
Honduras—Vice President Ricardo Tuniga Augustinus.
Britain—Ambassador Sir Patrick Dean.
France—Ambassador Charles Lucet.
West Germany—Ambassador Henrich Nappstein and West Berlin's Senator for Federal Affairs, Dietrich Spangenbert.

TV seeks out Ethel Kennedy even in her private goodbye.

NEW YORK (UPI) . . . Ethel Kennedy sat quiet and composed in the great Neo-Gothic Cathedral where 6 cardinals, 18 bishops and more than 200 priests conducted a solemn requiem mass for her slain husband.

Five hours earlier, when the last of the 151,000 mourners had passed the bier of her husband, Ethel Kennedy paid her own last visit. Arriving at St. Patrick's Cathedral before dawn, she sat in a chair near the end of the coffin and, placing her head in her hands, sat motionless for several minutes.

She stayed in the towering church for almost 40 minutes but it was not the private time she had hoped it would be. A television camera focused on her face and caught the lines of pain and hurt it bore.

President Johnson plays as subdued a role as possible.

by Merriman Smith

NEW YORK (UPI) . . . President Johnson, who clashed politically with Senator Robert F. Kennedy in life, knelt mourning for him today.

The President—visibly shaken by the assassination of the New York Senator—flew to New York to attend the high requiem mass.

Johnson, in a dark gray suit and accompanied by his wife, Lady Bird, was ushered to a front row pew in huge St. Patrick's Cathedral a few minutes before the mass began for the slain Senator.

The Johnsons sat immediately across the broad center aisle of the cathedral from the Kennedy family. The President's entrance through the 5th Avenue side of the cathedral was purposely unheralded. He and his wife walked virtually the full length of the church before the other mourners noticed them and rose out of respect.

Since the first news that Kennedy had been shot reached him, Johnson has played a subdued and helpful role to the family. He provided government aircraft to transport the Kennedys from the West Coast but has carefully sought to avoid anything approaching a dominant or prominent role in mourning ceremonies.

Aside from one public statement while doctors sought to save Kennedy's life, the President has remained out of the public eye.

Accompanied by two ranking staff members, Joseph Califano and James Jones, the President and Mrs. Johnson flew early Saturday to Floyd Bennett Field on Long Island, then by helicopter to Central Park. Then they were quickly escorted by limousine to the cathedral.

The President, whose religious denomination is the Disciples of Christ, frequently attends mass with his daughter, Mrs. Luci Nugent, at a small Catholic church near his Texas ranch.

When he entered the pew today, he knelt immediately, for a few mo-

Pallbearers carry the coffin from St. Patrick's after the requiem mass.

Funeral procession moves slowly along 34th Street and turns onto 7th Avenue on its way to Penn-Central Station.

ments of silent contemplation, as did Mrs. Johnson, who is an Episcopalian.

As the requiem mass ended, the Johnsons left quickly through a rear entrance of the church, stopping briefly at the family pew to say a few words of consolation to Mrs. Ethel Kennedy, widow of the Senator, and several of her children.

Mrs. Jacqueline Kennedy, widow of the late President John F. Kennedy, was seated at a spot where the President had no easy access, so he left the area near the altar and headed to the rear of the church with no further contact with the family.

Life goes on at St. Patrick's Cathedral.

NEW YORK (UPI) . . . Within minutes after the last guests left St. Patrick's Cathedral after the funeral of Senator Robert F. Kennedy Saturday, a crowd of several thousand waiting across the street surged into the church for the noon mass.

While sanitation men swept up litter along Fifth Avenue and television crews began to dismantle their platforms, hundreds of women searched the pews of the church for programs that might have been left behind.

Even before the barricades were all down, ice cream vendors crowded onto the sidewalk in front of the main entrance on Fifth Avenue. They did a booming business in Friday's 90-degree heat while people waited for up to six hours to pass the coffin of Robert F. Kennedy, but today they came overstocked.

Inside the dark cathedral the devout, the grief-stricken and the merely curious lit candles, wandered about, sat in pews or pushed into the small alcove where flowers had been put.

On one bouquet, a large cross in blue and white flowers, a silk ribbon had a message written in gold sequins. It read:

"We never forget you Bobby. From the Puerto Rican community."

Marilyn Dick, 12, who waited for six hours to see Kennedy's coffin Friday and then returned again Saturday, said she couldn't understand why anyone would have wanted to kill him.

"On television they said the man hated Israelis and that he might have wanted to kill Kennedy because Kennedy wanted to help them," she said. "I can't see any sense in that, killing a person because he wanted to help someone."

Ted Kennedy's Eulogy To His Brother

"Love is not an easy feeling to put into words."

The text of Senator Edward M. Kennedy's emotion-packed tribute to his brother that he addressed to the mourners at a requiem mass in St. Patrick's Cathedral follows:

Your eminences, your excellencies, Mr. President. In behalf of Mrs. Kennedy, her children, the parents and sisters of Robert Kennedy, I want to express what we feel to those who mourn with us today in this cathedral and around the world.

We loved him as a brother and as a father and as a son. From his parents and from his older brothers and sisters, Joe and Kathleen and Jack, he received an inspiration which he passed on to all of us.

He gave us strength in time of trouble, wisdom in time of uncertainty and sharing in time of happiness. He will always be by our side.

Love is not an easy feeling to put into words. Nor is loyalty or trust or joy. But he was all of these. He loved life completely and he lived it intensely.

A few years back Robert Kennedy wrote some words about his own father which expresses the way we in his family felt about him. He said of what his father meant to him, and I quote:

"What it really all adds up to is love. Not love as it is described with such facility in popular magazines, but the kind of love that is affection and respect, order and encouragement and support.

"Our awareness of this was an incalculable source of strength. And because real love is something unselfish and involves sacrifice and giving, we could not help but profit from it."

And he continued:

"Beneath it all he has tried to engender a social conscience. There were wrongs which needed attention, there were people who were poor and needed help, and we have a responsibility to them and this country.

"Through no virtues and accomplishments of our own, we have been fortunate enough to be born in the United States under the most comfortable condition. We therefore have a responsibility to others who are less well off."

That is what Robert Kennedy was given.

What he leaves to us is what he said, what he did and what he stood for.

A speech he made for the young people of South Africa on their day of affirmation in 1966 sums it up the best, and I would like to read it now.

"There is discrimination in this world and slavery and slaughter and starvation. Governments repress their people. Millions are trapped in poverty, while the nation grows rich and wealth is lavished on armaments everywhere.

"These are differing evils, but they are the common works of man. They reflect the imperfection of human justice, the inadequacy of human compassion, our lack of sensibility towards the suffering of our fellows.

"But we can perhaps remember, even if only for a time, that those who live with us are our brothers, that they share with us the same short moment of life, that they seek as we do nothing but the chance to live out their lives in purpose and happiness, winning what satisfaction and fulfillment they can.

"Surely this bond of common faith, this bond of common goals, can begin to teach us something. Surely we can learn at least to look at those around us as fellow men. And surely we can begin to work a little harder to bind up the wounds among us and to become in our own hearts brothers and countrymen once again.

"The answer is to rely on youth, not a time of life but a state of mind, a temper of the will, a quality of imagination, a predominance of courage over timidity, of the appetite for adventure over the love of ease. The cruelties and obstacles of this swiftly changing planet will not yield to the obsolete dogmas and outworn slogans; they cannot be moved by those who cling to a present that is already dying, who prefer the illusion of security to the excitement and danger that come with even the most peaceful progress.

"It is a revolutionary world which we live in, and this generation at home and around the world has had thrust upon it a greater burden of responsibility than any generation that has ever lived. Some believe there is nothing one man or one woman can do against the enormous array of

194

the world's ills. Yet many of the world's great movements of thought and action have flowed from the work of a single man.

"A young monk began the Protestant Reformation. A young general extended an empire from Macedonia to the borders of the earth. A young woman reclaimed the territory of France, and it was a young Italian explorer who discovered the New World, and the 32-year-old Thomas Jefferson who explained that all men are created equal.

"These men moved the world, and so can we all. Few will have the greatness to bend history itself, but each of us can work to change a small portion of events, and in the total of all those acts will be written the history of this generation.

"Each time a man stands for an ideal, or acts to improve the lot of others, or strikes out against injustice, he sends forth a tiny ripple of hope.

"And crossing each other from a million different centers of energy and daring, those ripples build a current that can sweep down the mightiest walls of oppression and resistance. Few are willing to brave the disapproval of their fellows, the censure of their colleagues, the wrath of their society. Moral courage is a rarer commodity than bravery in battle or great intelligence. Yet it is the one essential vital quality for those who seek to change a world that yields most painfully to change.

"And I believe that in this generation those with the courage to enter the moral conflict will find themselves with companions in every corner of the globe.

"For the fortunate among us there is the temptation to follow the easy and familiar paths of personal ambition and financial success so grandly spread before those who enjoy the privilege of education. But that is not the road history has marked out for us.

"Like it or not, we live in times of danger and uncertainty. But they are also more open to the creative energy of men than any other time in history. All of us will ultimately be judged and as the years pass, we will surely judge ourselves, on the effort we have contributed to building a new world society and the extent to which our ideals and goals have shaped that event.

"Our future may lie beyond our vision, but it is not completely beyond our control. It is the shaping impulse of America that neither faith nor nature nor the irresistible tides of history but the work of our own hands matched to reason and principle will determine our destiny."

There is pride in that, even arrogance, but there is also experience and truth, and in any event it is the only way we can live. That is the way he lived. That is what he leaves us.

My brother need not be idealized or enlarged in death beyond what he was in life. He should be remembered simply as a good and decent man who saw wrong and tried to right it, saw suffering and tried to heal it, saw war and tried to stop it.

Those of us who loved him and who take him to his rest today pray that what he was to us, and what he wished for others, will some day come to pass for all the world.

As he said many times, in many parts of this nation, to those he touched and who sought to touch him:

"Some men see things as they are and say why. I dream things that never were and say, why not."

Funeral Train

Slowed by crowds and tragedy, the final pil-grimage to Washington runs four hours late.

by Milton Benjamin, Ed Rogers, and Mike Feinsilber

ABOARD KENNEDY FUNERAL TRAIN (UPI) . . . The black-draped funeral train snaked through the June heat at a crawl carrying the flag-covered coffin of Robert F. Kennedy back to Washington.

"I have never seen anything like it in my life," the engineer of the funeral train, John P. Flanagan, 48, said. "There were thousands and thousands of people all over. The bell was rung continuously, I would say, from New York to Washington. The whistle was blown approaching every crowd. Everytime we came to a small town we had to bring the train down to 15 or 20 miles per hour."

Normally Flanagan makes the 226-mile run at 80 miles per hour and in a little more than four hours but Saturday it lasted from 1:02 p.m. when the train left Penn Central Station in New York, to 9:07 p.m., the time he clocked the Washington arrival.

The 21-car train came out of the tunnel from New York under the Hudson River and right away, in the middle of an old automobile junk-yard, you saw the people.

The balding, middle-aged man, wearing a dirty, sweat-stained under-shirt, was holding a battered felt hat over his heart. The woman standing next to him was waving a green kerchief with one hand and brushing away the tears with the other.

A mile farther down the tracks, two paunchy cops were standing stiffly at attention beside their squad car. They saluted the train smartly as it passed.

As the funeral train passes through cities and hamlets, Senator Edward M. Kennedy stands solemnly on the black-draped rear platform.

Waiting for the funeral train in Philadelphia.

FUNERAL AND BURIAL — SATURDAY, JUNE 8

More than a million Little Leaguers, Girl Scouts, service station attendants, veterans, bankers, bookkeepers, and ragpickers lined the tracks of the Penn-Central Railroad from New York to Washington Saturday to pay their final respects to Robert Francis Kennedy.

A little girl in a blue-and-white dress, sitting piggyback on her daddy's shoulders, waved a tiny American flag. An elderly woman, wearing a heavy cloth coat on a hot, sticky day, stood at the side of the tracks with a wilted rose.

As the train made its way through seamier sections of towns, men clutching bottles of beer and women in housecoats with their hair up in curlers lined the porches of the tenements.

In middle-class suburbs, they stood out on their back lawns—hollering at the kids to get out of the wading pool and not miss the brief glimpse of history.

They jammed the stations and overflowed onto the tracks, and in Elizabeth, N.J., a passenger train racing in the other direction struck and killed two mourners who didn't see the other train until it was too late.

They climbed water towers, hung from the girders of overpasses, and stood on the roofs of their cars to get a better view. And in one case, this also resulted in tragedy. A man who had climbed onto the roof of a box car grabbed the overhead wire to steady himself and was badly burned by the surge of electricity.

As the train crossed a river outside Newark, N.J., three firemen stood at attention on the deck of their fireboat. Its name, *The John F. Kennedy*.

Near Philadelphia, where a high-speed expressway ran alongside the tracks, hundreds of motorists illegally parked along the road. A few doubleparked—leaving their cars on the highway. Some raised their hoods in hopes the police would think the auto had broken down and wouldn't ticket them.

In the flatlands of New Jersey, someone had taken a can of black spray paint and written on a railroad overpass: "New Jersey is saddened."

The Rev. Ralph David Abernathy, wearing his dungaree suit and sipping iced tea, slumped in a seat on the train, looked out the window and said to his seatmate:

"I think this only goes to show there is a reservoir of goodwill in this country. We have seen more than a million people out there—black people, white people, brown and yellow people—and they are saying in their own way to the Kennedy family, and to Bobby, we love you."

The eight hours aboard the train to Washington became almost insufferable. The hoped-for gay love-of-life of an old Irish wake was lost, even though the Kennedys, of all people, went through the cars trying, of all

201

things, to raise the spirits of the 1,000 mourners.

The air conditioning was insufficient, the food went stale, but the bars were well stocked.

Joseph Kennedy III, 15, the oldest son of Robert Kennedy, went through each of the 21 cars, smiling bravely, shaking each hand saying, "Thank you for coming."

Ethel Kennedy left the casket and went through the cars with a word and a smile and a pat on the back. "I haven't seen you for so long," to one guest; "So nice you were able to make it," to another. "We'll cry later," she told someone else.

At Baltimore, near the end of the mournful journey, some 7,500 people held a memorial service on the railroad station platform. As the train rolled slowly through, they sang "The Battle Hymn of the Republic"— just as another Baltimore crowd had done when Abraham Lincoln's funeral train passed through the same city 103 years ago.

In Philadelphia, crowds began gathering at noon. By the time the tardy train rolled through North Philadelphia at 5 p.m., about 32,000 persons were jammed into the station and along embankments facing the tracks.

Some screamed, some sobbed, some tossed bouquets at the last car of the train, where Kennedy's flag-draped casket showed clearly through windows.

Kennedy's widow, most of his children, and the immediate family rode in the last two cars, with some of the world's most illustrious men and women in their company.

Ambassador W. Averell Harriman, former Secretary of Defense Robert S. McNamara, Lord Harlech of Great Britain, former Treasury Secretary C. Douglas Dillon, and Senator Edward M. Kennedy were all aboard and serving as active pall bearers.

New York Governor Nelson Rockefeller, Mayor and Mrs. John V. Lindsay of New York, Senators Charles Percy and Everett Dirksen of Illinois, Mrs. Martin Luther King Jr., civil rights leader Charles Evers, athletes Roosevelt Grier and Rafer Johnson were a few among the passengers comprising a "blue book" of American public life.

As the train arrived at Washington Union Station to be greeted by a 106-member honor guard of the armed services, a young woman standing on a hillside threw a bouquet of wild flowers underneath the wheels of the train as it slowly rolled past the hushed crowd.

Edward Kennedy, who had been on the platform of the rear observation car containing the casket, waving at well-wishers, moved inside at the end of the journey to stand at the head of the coffin with his hands crossed and his head bowed.

Throngs lined the railroad tracks from New York to Washington, D.C. In Elizabeth, N.J., TV cameras focus on the tragedy of a northbound express plowing into the crowd.

Kennedy mourners killed
by express train.

ELIZABETH, N.J. (UPI) . . . A 3-year-old girl was hospitalized Sunday in fair condition, one of the victims of an accident which killed two persons and injured five others waiting on railroad tracks to view the Robert F. Kennedy funeral train.

Debra Ann Kwiatek of Linden was being treated for back injuries and cuts at Elizabeth General Hospital.

The child's grandmother, Mrs. Antoinette Sevirini, and John Curia, both 56 and of Elizabeth, were killed when a northbound passenger train brushed spectators looking the other direction for the funeral train.

Treated at St. Elizabeth's hospital and released were Mrs. Magdeline Cockerhan, 32; Joanne Rzepka, 16; and Mrs. Ingrid Goves, 19, all suffering shock; and Mrs. Genevieve Murphy, who sustained a broken hand and was treated for shock. All are from Elizabeth. Two other persons also were injured in accidents at other points along the tragedy-marred and much-delayed 226 mile procession from New York.

Edward Bowers, 37, an Elizabeth factory worker, said he was standing on the tracks with the victims when the northbound Chicago-to-New York express "The Admiral" roared through Elizabeth.

"I grabbed Mrs. Sevirini's hand and tried to pull her out of the way," he said, "but it was too late. The train was moving about 60 miles an hour. It all happened too quick."

Bores said he pushed his wife, Doris, 37, to safety but the train struck the Kwiatek child. "She was spinning around like a top," Bores said. Debra's father, Adam Kwiatek, 25, managed to leap from the path of the oncoming train.

About 5,000 persons were waiting at the station to watch the Kennedy train and the air stream following the express rocked many off balance as it whizzed by. The accident happened just after the streamliner rounded a curve, its whistle blaring.

Elizabeth is not an express stop. The accident stopped northbound traffic—and the Kennedy train—for a period. Mayor Thomas Dunn earlier had cautioned the crowds to remain off the tracks.

David E. Smucker, Penn Central executive vice president for railroad operations, said in a statement the train "which struck the spectators was taking special safety precautions.

"It was moving about half its regular speed, as a precautionary measure, when it came out of the S-curve at Elizabeth. . . ."

Smucker said the engineer reduced his speed from 55 miles an hour to about 30 miles an hour, "and he was repeatedly sounding" the train bell. He said the engineer applied the brakes when he saw people on the tracks but that the crush of the crowds kept the victims from getting out of the way.

Cardinal Cushing flown back to Boston by Air Force.

BOSTON (UPI) . . .Richard Cardinal Cushing, who became ill aboard the Kennedy funeral train, was returned to Boston Saturday night aboard an Air Force jet. The Cardinal, who has been ailing in recent years, was not hospitalized.

A chancery spokesman said the 72-year-old prelate had gone to bed at his residence before midnight.

Two doctors were summoned to Union Station in Washington to meet him on arrival but the Cardinal walked off the train unassisted to a waiting car.

There were no doctors aboard the jet that brought the Cardinal to Boston. "Just his own people," an Air Force spokesman said. "He was perfectly all right," the spokesman added.

Cushing, a long time friend of the Kennedy family, had been scheduled to participate in the graveside ceremony in Washington.

The Cardinal was flown to Boston in a Lockheed Jetstar, a VIP plane, from Andover Air Force Base in Maryland.

Other Memorable Funeral Trains.

WASHINGTON (UPI) . . . Washington has often been a terminal for special funeral trains bearing the bodies of notable dead, including three assassinated Presidents.

The first carried the body of President Abraham Lincoln from Washington to Springfield, Ill., in 1865.

In September, 1881, a special train brought the body of President James A. Garfield, from Elberon, N.J., to Washington, to lie in state. Another train then took the body to Cleveland, Ohio, for burial.

President William McKinley was shot Sept. 6, 1901, in Buffalo, N.Y. A special funeral train brought his body to Washington to lie in state, and another transported his casket to Canton, Ohio.

When President Warren G. Harding died in San Francisco on Aug. 2,

In Vatican City, Pope Paul VI prays for the soul of Robert F. Kennedy.

1923, a special train carried his body across the nation to Washington. His casket was then taken by train to Marion, Ohio, for burial.

A special train brought the body of President Franklin Delano Roosevelt to Washington after he died in Warm Springs, Ga., on April 12, 1945. After lying in state, his body was carried to Hyde Park, N.Y., for interment.

Lincoln and Kennedy funeral trains passed through many of same cities.

CHICAGO (UPI) . . . Thousands of mourners waited somberly in depots of cities big and small 103 years ago to pay their respects to another assassinated American leader whose body was also borne to its final resting place by train.

Large crowds waited on the platforms of railroad stations from Washington to Springfield, Ill., for the train bearing the body of President Abraham Lincoln. The only member of the Lincoln family aboard the train returning his body to Springfield for burial was a son, Robert Todd, 23, according to newspaper clippings on file at the Chicago Historical Society. Mrs. Lincoln remained behind in the White House, "prostrate in shock."

Lincoln's casket was in the second car from the rear. Near it was another coffin containing the body of Lincoln's son, Willie, who died at the age of 12. It had been removed from a vault in a Washington cemetery to be buried with the boy's father at Oak Ridge Cemetery in Springfield.

The two funeral corteges, separated by more than a century in time, passed through some of the same cities between Washington and New York. The Lincoln cortege went from New York City to Albany, then west through Syracuse and Rochester, N.Y., across the northwest corner of Pennsylvania, through Ohio, and Indiana to Chicago before turning south to Springfield for the last leg of the sorrowful journey.

Lincoln's coffin was put on public view in 10 cities during the 12-day 1,650-mile trip that ended in Springfield at 9 a.m. May 3, 1865.

Laid To Rest

*Solemn ceremony concludes four
emotion-racked days.*

by Louis Cassels

ARLINGTON, VA. (UPI) . . . Angry black clouds cleared Saturday night and Robert Francis Kennedy was laid to rest by the light of flickering candles and a spring moon within sight of the eternal flame over the grave of his brother, John F. Kennedy.

A day of national sorrow and desolation of spirit that began with a funeral mass before thousands at St. Patrick's Cathedral in New York City ended on the hushed, rain-dampened slopes of Arlington National Cemetery, shrine of the honored dead.

A light rain began to fall before the funeral train bearing the Senator's body pulled into Union Station from New York City.

A solemn President Johnson was at the train station to meet the cortege of mourners when they arrived.

Ted Kennedy walked just ahead of the casket as it was borne from the train to the hearse.

President Johnson shook hands with Ted and other members of the family. The President then stood silent while the Navy hymn was played. Vice President Hubert H. Humphrey, who arrived at Union Station with the Chief Executive, stood with hat in hand at the opposite side of the rear of the hearse. The casket was loaded between them.

Two sailors, each bearing a rifle with fixed bayonet, faced each other across the casket.

The door of the hearse was closed on the casket upon completion of

the Navy hymn at 9:35 p.m. The family and crowd of friends and dignitaries then filed slowly through a jammed area to the black limousines
that had been parked near the hearse.

Ethel Kennedy and one of her sons entered the front of the hearse. A
moment later, Mrs. Kennedy stepped out briefly to greet House Speaker
John W. McCormack. Ted Kennedy joined Mrs. Kennedy, her son, and
the driver in the front seat of the hearse.

Several thousand persons who had waited for hours alongside the
Senate Office Buildings fell silent as the cortege drove between the new
and old Senate Office Buildings.

Darkness had fallen long since, and most of those who had waited so
long could make out no single individual in the official party.

The crowd, repeatedly dampened and then dried again by intermittent
showers during the long wait, dispersed quietly after the cortege passed.

Moving to the cemetery, the hearse paused momentarily on Constitution Avenue in front of the Justice Department, where Kennedy served as
Attorney General while his brother was President.

Attorney General Ramsey Clark and his wife waited in front of the
building for 45 minutes for the funeral procession. One of the cars in the
procession stopped to pick up the Clarks to take them to Arlington National Cemetery.

At the Lincoln Memorial, the U.S. Army hearse bearing Kennedy's body
stopped while a choir sang "The Battle Hymn Of The Republic" and the
poor people of adjacent Resurrection City—the Senator's special consti-
tuency—reached out into the dark with uplifted hands.

Television cameras focused on two raised, clasped hands. One was
white and one was black.

The hearse paused briefly as it passed the reflecting pool alongside
Resurrection City. The pool, which stretches between the Washington
Monument and the Lincoln Memorial, reflected a bright late spring moon
that shone through fast-departing thunderclouds.

Shortly before the cortege was expected to arrive at the cemetery, army
officers distributed candles to the specially invited guests and members of
the diplomatic corps. The guests and the diplomats held the candles in
their hands without lighting them.

But farther down the hillside where the general public was waiting,
hundreds of candles were lighted among the dark trees which stood out
sharply against the moonlit sky.

Among those diplomats who took a candle—and subsequently lighted it
—was Soviet Ambassador Anatoly Dobryin.

By the time the funeral cortege was crossing Memorial Bridge, the
weather which had been threatening at the cemetery was much better. A

Hearse bearing Kennedy's body passes the nation's Capitol on the way to Arlington National Cemetery.

At the Lincoln Memorial a delegation of Poor People campaigners from Resurrection City salutes the slain hero with upraised hands.

Robert F. Kennedy Jr. leads pallbearers as they carry the casket to the grave-site. Clockwise from the left are Stephen Smith, brother-in-law of Senator Kennedy; John Seigenthaler, a former aide; LeMoyne Billings, a family friend; mountaineer James Whittaker, (partially obscured); W. Averell Harriman, chief negotiator of the Vietnam peace talks; Olympic athlete Rafer Johnson; former

Secretary of the Treasury C. Douglas Dillon (at extreme right rear); Bill Barry, a Kennedy aide; astronaut John Glenn (almost completely obscured); former British Ambassador to the U.S. Lord Harlech; former Secretary of Defense Robert McNamara, and David Hackett, a family friend.

Space hero John Glenn passes the folded flag that had draped the casket to Senator Edward Kennedy.

Holding flickering candles, members of the Kennedy family kneel in prayer at the casket.

The Kennedy family leaves the gravesite at the conclusion of the rites.

Lights blaze at the gravesite below the Custis-Lee Mansion high on a hill in Arlington National Cemetery.

bright nearly full moon shone in the sky.

The hearse arrived at the base of the Kennedy Memorial—marked by its famous eternal flame—at 10:24 p.m. That meant the funeral was almost exactly five hours behind schedule.

The black military hearse pulled up at the foot of a walkway leading up to the gravesite.

The pallbearers gathered around the hearse and prepared to carry the coffin the distance of no less than 100 yards uphill to the grave. Around it sparkled thousands of small tapers.

As the ceremony started President Johnson stood at the far left and behind the Kennedy family group of Edward Kennedy, his wife Joan, and Mrs. Ethel Kennedy.

One of Kennedy's dogs—Freckles, an Irish spaniel that he had sometimes taken campaigning with him—lunged against his leash, trying to get to his master's coffin.

Some of the Kennedy children carried flowers and some of them also carried candles. The graveside ceremony was a simple religious one, without military trappings. The Kennedy family had requested that there be no gun salutes or troops.

The final, brief burial liturgy was said by Archbishop Philip M. Hannan of New Orleans, a family friend who substituted for Richard Cardinal Cushing of Boston, stricken ill during the funeral train ride to Washington.

The ceremony at the gravesite took only about 15 minutes. There was no military fanfare. No bugler, no guns.

After the prayers were said the pallbearers returned to the casket, removed the American flag and folded it. The Harvard University band began playing "America."

The Kennedy family stood quietly, motionlessly. Astronaut John Glenn, serving as a pallbearer, handed the flag to Ted Kennedy. Ted handed it to Joseph P. Kennedy III, 15, eldest son of the slain Senator, who gave it in turn to his dazed mother.

Ted Kennedy then led the Senator's widow over to President Johnson. She appeared to whisper just a few words in the President's ear. Then they all turned and walked back down the hill.

The pallbearers lifted the coffin and carried it the few feet to the spot where it would be lowered into the ground later after the mourners had left.

One by one, the Kennedy family, adults and children, knelt to kiss the mahogany casket at the end of its journey, under a magnolia tree 60 feet southeast of the late President's grave.

A solemn President and Mrs. Johnson silently shook hands with the widow and left, followed by the grieving family and their friends, govern-ment officials, and foreign diplomats.

As the crowd was leaving several members of it, one or two at a time, came forward to kneel for a moment by the casket.

At first only two persons did this, then two more, then four, then a dozen or so.

So ended the latest tragic chapter in the Kennedy story. It was 12 weeks to the day since Robert F. Kennedy had embarked on his quest for the Presidency because, he said, "I am convinced that this country is on a perilous course."

The poor mourn Kennedy.

by Richard Lerner

WASHINGTON (UPI) . . . Poor People's campaigners put aside internal problems Saturday to join in final tribute to Senator Robert F. Kennedy.

Twenty-five residents of the shantytown were invited by the Kennedy family to ride in the final procession of the funeral day, taking the body of the slain Senator and champion of causes of the poor from Union Station to Arlington Cemetery.

Hosea Williams, the principal organizer of activities by the Resurrec-tion City inhabitants, asked the others to pay their respects to Kennedy by lining half the circle around the Lincoln Memorial as the procession passed.

The camptown of plywood and plastic huts is located between lines of trees right by the memorial. Most residents had to walk only a short distance, a matter of a few yards for some, to take up the vigil for view-ing the last mile of Senator Kennedy's last journey.

In the grief over Kennedy's death, even the capture of the accused assassin of the martyred father of the Poor People's campaign, the Rev. Martin Luther King Jr., brought little satisfaction to the Resurrection City residents.

Informed of the arrest in London of James Earl Ray, Williams said, "Fine—but I am not at near concerned about him as I am worried about the system that produced him. We are concerned with a sick and evil society which produces violence." He added: "Millions must understand that it is this society that killed President Kennedy, Malcolm X, Martin Luther King, and Robert Kennedy."

The Kennedy funeral and the Ray capture temporarily overshadowed internal problems of march leaders. They were trying to get Sterling Tucker, a Washington Negro leader, to accept the directorship of a June 19 demonstration that is to climax the campaign.

Bayard Rustin, who coordinated the Dr. King-led 1963 march on Washington, quit in a dispute over goals. He outlined several days ago what he called a realistic list of objectives for the campaign, but Williams subsequently disavowed them.

The Rev. Ralph David Abernathy, head of the march, sided with Williams, so Rustin quit.

Echoes from Kennedy's life.

WASHINGTON (UPI) . . . The dolorous funeral cortege that carried the body of Robert F. Kennedy through the avenues of Washington Saturday night caught echoes from his life.

From Washington's Union Station, the hearse and auto procession passed by the Old Senate Office Building.

In its Caucus Room last March 16, Kennedy said in announcing he was a candidate for the Presidency: "I do not run for the Presidency merely to oppose any man but to propose new policies. I run because I am convinced that this country is on a perilous course and because I have such strong feelings about what must be done that I am obliged to do all I can."

In the New Senate Office Building where he had his office was the Senate Judiciary Committee Hearing Room where he said in 1963 while testifying as Attorney General on a civil rights bill:

"This legislation should be enacted to bring to law what we have always known in our hearts to be justice."

He also spoke of outbreaks of violence by Negro demonstrators in the cities.

"We cannot excuse violence from any source or from any group," the young Attorney General said. "The responsibility of the Negro leaders who set these demonstrations in motion is very great as is the responsibility of the white leadership in every community. But our responsibility as a nation is most plain. We must remove the injustices."

The procession turned down from Capitol Hill toward Arlington National Cemetery. En route, it passed the Justice Department where he had served as Attorney General when his assassinated brother John was President.

223

It was from that government command post that he sent U.S. marshals to the University of Mississippi to protect James Meredith in the bloody battle over the admission of the young Negro to the school.

It was in his Cabinet office there that someone once brought him a clipping sniping at a minor prosecution conducted by the Justice Department under his supervision.

"I don't give a damn what they say," he said. "It's right and that's all there is to it."

Jacqueline and children visit JFK's grave.

ARLINGTON, VA. (UPI) . . . Mrs. Jacqueline Kennedy led her two children, Caroline and John, in paying homage at the grave of her late husband in Arlington National Cemetery Saturday night after services for her slain brother-in-law.

The three of them, ringed by candle-bearing mourners, knelt before the marker at President John F. Kennedy's grave, which is about 60 feet from Robert Kennedy's final resting place.

The crowd was large and the incident was marked with high emotional tension but there was complete silence as the solemn salute was made.

Mrs. Kennedy has visited the site only on rare occasions and mostly when she could have maximum privacy since President Kennedy's assassination in 1963.

The former First Lady, slim and solemn in pure black; Caroline in white; and John, in a white shirt and short dark trousers, walked almost around the circular monument to the late President to get inside it.

She and the children knelt before the bronze marker, in the full glare of television lights and before hundreds of spectators as well as millions watching in their homes, and bowed their heads with their arms resting on part of the chain barrier surrounding the grave.

They selected flowers from a small floral plot beside the marker and placed them on the late President's grave and the graves of two of his children who died shortly after birth.

Eulogy at the Department of Justice.

WASHINGTON (UPI) . . . About 250 persons gathered in the inner courtyard of the Justice Department Saturday to eulogize former Attorney

Jacqueline Kennedy and her children Caroline and John Jr. pause to pray at the grave of President John F. Kennedy.

General Robert F. Kennedy and then lined Constitution Avenue outside to watch his funeral procession.

Attorney General Ramsey Clark, whom Kennedy appointed head of the department's Lands Division in 1961, said the New York Senator "started like a sprinter and he proved himself like a long-distance runner."

"Bob Kennedy stood for a life as few among us have," Clark added. "It is thus we must always remember him."

Archibald Cox, a Harvard Law School professor who was U.S. Solicitor General under Kennedy, said the Senator proved that "the revolution of social and economic justice" can be achieved.

Harold H. Greene, a former department civil rights lawyer who now is chief judge of the District of Columbia Court of General Sessions, said he found Kennedy "compassionate and considerate."

"The private man Kennedy was much more gentle, more patient and more shy than the public realized," Greene said.

Army passed out the candles.

WASHINGTON (UPI) . . . The hundeds of candles that flickered at the burial rites for Robert F. Kennedy Saturday night were a hastily-arranged improvisation.

As the Kennedy funeral train made its slow journey from New York to Washington, someone aboard realized that it would arrive far behind schedule, requiring the Arlington National Cemetery ceremony to be held after nightfall.

Deputy Secretary of State Nicholas Katzenbach called ahead from the Kennedy funeral train about the candles. He called his State Department office, which relayed his request to the Defense Department.

In the two hours it had, the department found about a thousand candles at the Catholic Archdiocese of Washington. "I can assure you it was frantic," said one official involved in the candle hunt.

The tapers were distributed to the funeral party as it arrived at the grave site by members of the 1st Battalion, 3rd Infantry, which serves as an honor guard at Arlington.

Upwelling of grief knows no boundaries.

LONDON (UPI) . . . Thousands of Europeans paid last respects to Robert F. Kennedy Saturday with prayers in holy places and signatures in black condolence books placed in American embassies and consulates.

The grief stretched from London to Western Europe and across the Iron Curtain into the communist nations of Yugoslavia and Bulgaria.

In Vatican City, American priests and young men studying for the priesthood knelt around Pope Paul VI as the Pontiff held a special prayer service in his private chapel. A mass for the repose of Kennedy's soul was celebrated in Rome at Santa Susanna Church, the American parish in the Eternal City.

In Belgrade, Premier Mika Spiljak led more than 3,000 Yugoslavs in signing a condolence book for Kennedy in the lobby of the U.S. Embassy.

Prime Minister Todor Zhivkov sent a message of sympathy to Mrs. Ethel Kennedy from the Bulgarian capital of Sofia, expressing the shock on behalf of his people and the communist government.

The line of mourners outside the U.S. embassy in London stretched for blocks.

President Eamon De Valera led grief-stricken Ireland, the nation of Kennedy's ancestors, in a pontifical requiem mass for the fallen Senator in Dublin Cathedral.

The universality of grief was underscored in London where Dr. Immanuel Jakobovits, Britain's chief rabbi, paid tribute to Kennedy in a sermon at St. John's Wood Synagogue.

"This evil deed has disgraced not only America," the rabbi said of the assassination. "It has shamed the entire human race."

Corneliu Manescu, President of the U.N. General Assembly, said the life and work of Senator Robert F. Kennedy were closely connected with the principles of the United Nations.

Manescu, also Foreign Minister of Romania and the first communist chief of the General Assembly, said in a sympathy message to Mrs. Ethel Kennedy:

"We were grieved to learn the sad news of the death of your husband, the eminent statesman, Senator Robert F. Kennedy.

"His tragic end has caused great sorrow at the United Nations, whose mission is to help insure that the world, safe from threats and acts of brutality, moves forward constructively and steadily, with full respect for the freedom of every man and every community, toward the ideals of peace and progress, principles with which the life and work of Robert F. Kennedy have been so closely connected.

"Please allow me to convey to you, as President of the General Assembly of the United Nations and in my personal capacity, our profound sympathy and our most sincere condolences."

Every detail for the funeral was worked out with Kennedy precision — even to spare railroad engines.

by Daniel Rapoport

WASHINGTON (UPI) . . . The thinking and energy of his family, campaign aides, old associates, railroad officials and countless local authorities went into the funeral of Robert F. Kennedy.

The federal government played a relatively minor supporting role.

Most of the myriad details were worked out by the Presidential campaign organization which carried the New York Senator through the primaries in Indiana, Nebraska, Oregon, South Dakota, and California.

To a newsman who had covered Kennedy through the primaries and who accompanied his body from California to New York and Washington, the logistics involved in the funeral and burial were "an extension of the campaign."

Superimposed over brother-in-law Stephen Smith's political organization were the commanding figures of former Defense Secretary Robert S. McNamara, another brother-in-law, Sargent Shriver, and other New Frontier figures.

McNamara, now president of the World Bank, applied his organizing genius to the task of quickly developing a smooth plan of operation.

Shriver, former Peace Corps director and antipoverty chief and now Ambassador to Paris, utilized his powers of persuasion and tact to implement the plan.

The 2,300 guests and dignitaries at the services at St. Patrick's Cathedral in New York were admitted by ticket or the 75-word telegrams sent out to all attending. Secretaries followed up each telegram with a personal phone call.

Staff workers, numb with grief from the shooting Wednesday morning, swung into action shortly after Kennedy died early Thursday.

Arrangements were made to transport about 150 news personnel from California to New York. Aides contacted officials of the Penn Central Railroad Thursday and worked out the family's wish for a funeral train from New York to Washington.

New York City police, Secret Service agents and railroad police combed Penn Station and the train that was to make the journey. To old railroad hands, the security was tighter than for any Presidential trip in memory.

Other Kennedy aides were in touch with St. Patrick's and the Archdiocese of New York to arrange for Friday's all-day vigil and Saturday's funeral service.

The Saturday service started right on schedule at 10 a.m. Newsmen were given mimeographed sheets explaining to non-Catholics every point in the service.

Meanwhile, hundreds of Penn Central officials and employees were strung out along the 226-mile route between Washington and New York, geared for any contingency. Joining them were local police who were asked to station men at every underpass and overhead bridge.

Preceding and following the 21-car train were spare engines, on hand in the event of a breakdown. An extra engineer was assigned to the train.

The trip to Washington took about four hours longer than anticipated, but the Kennedys had wanted it to travel slowly wherever people had come to pay their respects.

Except for a stretch of forest between Washington and Baltimore, the train never went beyond 30 miles an hour as thousands stood along the right of way and stared at the funeral car, the last one on the train.

After the service, buses that had transported train passengers from Union Station to Arlington National Cemetery took them to the Shoreham Hotel where they picked up their baggage. For those living outside Washington, the Kennedy staff had arranged for hotel rooms or transportation home.

Virtually the entire expense of the funeral and burial was borne by the Kennedys—including approximately $15,000 for the train. Federal expenses were limited to security needs.

The city of Washington, programmed for such events, had its police force augmented by National Guardsmen.

The Accused Assassin

*Listens to radio music
during Kennedy funeral.*

by Jack V. Fox

LOS ANGELES (UPI) . . . While millions of Americans watched television coverage of the funeral of Senator Robert F. Kennedy and his slow journey by train to a grave in Arlington National Cemetery, his accused assassin listened to soft music on a jail infirmary radio.

Jailers said there were no television sets in the second floor hospital ward where Sirhan Bishara Sirhan is lodged, and that radio music broadcast over a loudspeaker was not interrupted by news programs. Newspapers were distributed in the ward, and deputies said Sirhan probably had seen photographs of the funeral of the man he is accused of killing in the kitchen of the Ambassador Hotel early June 5.

A. L. Wirin, chief counsel for the Southern California branch of the American Civil Liberties Union, who has visited Sirhan daily in his cell, said he planned to go to court within the next few days to seek a court order for a "Big Name" attorney for the suspect.

Wirin's motion for "one or more outstanding lawyers" to be appointed for Sirhan was rejected by Superior Court Judge Arthur Alarcon at the arraignment, but the judge indicated he might reconsider the request later.

A representative of the Public Defender's office has been appointed to defend the former racetrack exercise boy, but Wirin hoped an attorney of the caliber of Melvin Belli, who defended Jack Ruby, would be sought by the court.

As Wirin passed Sirhan at the conclusion of the arraignment, the suspect hissed, "Money, money."

Wirin said Sirhan was reminding him he had asked that $300 of the $400 he was carrying when he was arrested be turned over to his mother,

Mrs. Mary Sirhan. Wirin said Sirhan wanted the rest of the money made available to him to buy personal necessities in jail.

Authorities believe the four $100 bills Sirhan carried the night of the assassination were part of the money he received four months ago in settlement of a disability claim for injuries from a fall from a horse.

Sirhan claimed he suffered head, back and eye injuries Sept. 25, 1966, when he fell off a filly he was exercising at the Rancho Granja Vista del Rio in Corona, Calif. Eye specialists who examined him reported no indication of impaired vision, but a neurosurgeon testified he could not tell if Sirhan had sustained a genuine head injury.

Sirhan was held under security so severe that he has not received a visit from a single member of his family. He was under constant surveillance in a bullet-proof second floor cell of the hospital section of the Los Angeles County Jail. An unarmed deputy was constantly in the room with him and an armed guard watched through a plastic door peephole.

The one-time racetrack exercise boy and aspiring jockey was not scheduled to appear in public until June 28, when a plea is to be entered on his behalf by the Public Defender's office.

Judge Alarcon also appointed two psychiatrists to examine the defendant and advise the defense in determining whether to enter an insanity plea which could save Sirhan from the gas chamber. Alarcon stressed that he was making no hint of judgment on Sirhan's sanity.

Los Angeles police questioned and quickly released three women—one a belly dancer — who voluntarily appeared, each saying she believed she was the "girl in the polka dot dress" sought after the shooting early Wednesday morning.

A Kennedy volunteer worker had said such a woman ran from the hotel saying, "We shot him," minutes after the Senator was fatally wounded. The police investigation was continuing on every lead. Officers said they were thoroughly checking every angle to determine if there had been a conspiracy.

Jordanian grocer may have been slain in revenge for Kennedy assassination.

CHICAGO (UPI) . . . A Jordanian grocer was shot to death in his South Side store Saturday in a slaying which might have been retaliation for the assassination of Senator Robert F. Kennedy, police said.

The victim was Abder Rayyan, 55, who was slain before the eyes of his nephew and daughter and 11 customers.

Police said they have been unable to determine any motive for the slaying but it might have been an abortive robbery or revenge for the killing of Kennedy.

Two Negro men walked into the store, which Rayyan had purchased only two months ago. Rayyan was at work at a rear counter, standing over a vegetable bin. One of the men walked up to him, drew a .38 caliber revolver and fired two shots. One of the bullets struck Rayyan behind the left ear.

Rayyan's daughter, Zuhdeia, 22, said the two men ran out of the store and down the street to a car parked about a block away. Waiting in the car were several other young men. The group drove away.

Rayyan was the father of nine children. He came to the United States five years ago from South America. Authorities said he left Jordan 16 years ago. His widow and other members of the family live in Quito, Ecuador.

Police were checking out reports that after the Kennedy assassination a rumor spread through the neighborhood around the store at 343 E. 51st St. that Rayyan had said, "Kennedy should have been dead long ago."

However, Rayyan apparently was an admirer of the Kennedy family. On the wall of his store was a poster with pictures of Presidents Abraham Lincoln and John F. Kennedy, and Dr. Martin Luther King Jr., inscribed, "They died to make men free."

Kennedy surgeon says half an inch would have saved Senator's life.

NEW YORK (UPI) . . . Dr. Henry M. Cuneo, the operating surgeon on slain Senator Robert F. Kennedy, says in the latest issue of *Time* magazine that, had the bullet struck one centimeter (less than half an inch) to the rear, the Senator's life would have been spared.

Cuneo, in an interview in the June 14 issue, said that, had that been the case, "the Senator would have been in good condition."

"But it hit the mastoid, which is a spongy honeycomb bone," Cuneo said. "Behind that is the thickest part of your head. That's solid. That little bullet would have just bounced off. But hitting the mastoid, it sent bone fragments all over the Senator's brain."

During the hours following the operation when the doctors failed to see any signs of consciousness, Cuneo said, "We were certain that the future would be disastrous for the Senator if he did survive."

He added that he did not tell Mrs. Kennedy about this theory. "I just told her we were doing everything we could," he said.

THE NATION MEDITATES

Sunday, June 9, 1968

Day of Mourning

President Johnson observes day of mourning in special White House services led by Evangelist Billy Graham.

by Mike Feinsilber

WASHINGTON (UPI) . . . Mrs. Ethel Kennedy and Mrs. Jacqueline Kennedy—and tens of thousands of their fellow Americans—mourned Robert Kennedy at his grave Sunday.

Observing the day of mourning he had proclaimed, President Johnson stayed in the White House with his family and attended a private service conducted by evangelist Billy Graham.

Thousands of persons were waiting outside the gate when Arlington Cemetery opened at 8 a.m. Under a cruel sun, they filed past the fresh sod, marked by a simple white, wooden cross, throughout the day.

At 11:34 Saturday night, after most of the mourners were gone, the mahogany casket bearing the body of the assassinated Senator was lowered into an underground vault, which was sealed and then covered with sod. Frank Mankiewicz, press secretary to Senator Kennedy, said the gravesite was temporary. The Kennedy family will choose a permanent site near the John F. Kennedy grave and will select a "very simple" monument.

Shortly after 10 a.m., Ethel Kennedy, accompanied by her oldest son, Joseph Kennedy III, 15, arrived. Carrying small bouquets of flowers, they went to the grave, knelt and prayed for about five minutes. The 15 honor guards sealed the area for the moment to allow them privacy.

About two hours later, Jacqueline Kennedy, her two children, John Jr.

and Caroline, and her sister and brother-in-law, Princess Lee Radziwill and Stanislas Radziwill, went to the grave of John F. Kennedy. The three Kennedys stood, silently and unnoticed by the throng, in the shade of a Japanese magnolia tree for several minutes

Then Jacqueline Kennedy and John Jr. went to the Senator's grave, 60 feet removed from the eternal flame marking the resting place of President Kennedy. They laid flowers at the foot of the grave and returned to the President's grave, on which Caroline placed a bouquet. Then they walked up the sloping, grassy knoll toward the Robert E. Lee mansion at its crest, and left.

Bells tolled in Washington and were heard in Arlington.

So numerous were the ordinary citizens who crossed the Potomac and went to Arlington, and waited in long lines in temperatures in the 80's, that members of the honor guard had to regulate the flow of mourners.

"They were all but stepping in the grave" of President Kennedy, Sgt. Morris W. Moore said. "They were waiting outside the gates when we opened at 8 o'clock this morning and they've been coming faster and faster all day."

Memorial services were held all over America.

Mrs. Rose Kennedy, 77, who has lost three sons—one in war and two to assassins—attended two masses here at St. Patrick's Cathedral. Then she returned to Hyannis Port, Mass., to comfort her husband, who suffered a stroke several years ago.

At the White House service, 22 persons attended. They included members of the President's staff and a few of his friends.

In his proclamation Thursday, Johnson asked Americans to observe Sunday with prayers and said: "The tragedy and senseless violence of Robert F. Kennedy's death casts a deep shadow of grief across America and the world."

During the past week, the President has tried to stay out of the public eye, but he attended both the funeral in New York and the burial in Washington.

Maury Wills of Pittsburgh and Rusty Staub and Bob Aspromonte of Houston risked possible fines when they refused to play in the Pirates-Astro game at Houston out of respect to Kennedy. Members of the New York Yankees and California Angels lined up in silent tribute along the baselines in Yankee Stadium.

Longshoremen and warehousemen held work stoppages at all California ports in memory of Kennedy.

In Kennedy's native state, an interfaith service was held on board the battleship Massachusetts, which is docked permanently at Fall River, Mass. In next door Rhode Island, services were conducted at the New-

Robert Kennedy's widow and oldest son kneel before the simple cross that marks the temporary grave at Arlington.

port Naval Base in memory of Kennedy and also the 99 crewmen aboard the missing submarine Scorpion.

John Cardinal Cody celebrated a special memorial mass at Quigley Seminary on Chicago's near North Side, while the annual Rock River conference of the Methodist Church at Dekalb, Ill., opened with a memorial prayer for Kennedy. All Greek Orthodox churches in the Midwest were asked to hold special services.

Michigan Lieutenant Governor William Milliken and Secretary of State James Cavanagh led a group of state and city officials attending a mass in Detroit conducted by Archbishop John Dearden.

At the Washington Episcopal Cathedral, the Very Rev. Francis B. Sayre Jr. said the trouble with America is not "sickness," but "old-fashioned sin."

In neglect of God's commandments, he said, Americans are giving way to "hatred, malice, selfishness, arrogance, and hasty violence which cuts down the flower of our manhood."

Mankiewicz said members of the Kennedy clan were bearing up well, "as they usually do."

"They're remarkable people," he said.

Ethel and the 10 children are expected to leave some time this month for the family's summer home on Cape Cod, where Kennedy sailed, swam and played with them.

Bobby Jr., 14, who helped carry his father's body to its final resting place Saturday, appeared most distraught. One of his instructors at Georgetown Prep in Washington described him as a "very nervous boy." Eleven-year-old daughter Courtney was reported "crushed."

Mankiewicz said he now will begin closing up the Kennedy-for-President headquarters here and try to find jobs for those employed in the campaign.

"We're closing down the juggernaut," he said in reference to a term used in some early press accounts of Robert Kennedy's bid for the Presidency.

Other Kennedy aides will be closing out Kennedy's official affairs as a Senator, and disposing of his office files.

In city where Kennedy was slain, tens of thousands attend memorial services.

LOS ANGELES (UPI) . . . The people of Los Angeles flocked to churches Sunday and freeways were bright with burning headlights in tribute to the Senator.

A massive crowd overflowed St. Vibiana's Cathedral for a solemn requiem mass presided over by James Francis Cardinal McIntyre at which Monsignor Patrick J. Roche delivered the eulogy.

"The fresh green fields of spring are now salted with humanity's tears and through them, looking up meekly, we search for reasons which explain the mystery of God's design," Roche said.

"Part of that design must be this: that our nation needed still another lesson of the tragedy contained in violence and strife. Two glaring lessons had already been given us in recent memory and yet there has been no healing of the nation's wounds.

"This may well be the final lesson given to us. We must learn as individuals and as groups that civic disorder, social antagonisms and personal hatreds pave the way of a nation's doom."

Thousands, many of them Negroes and Mexican-Americans, assembled for an interfaith rally at Wrigley Field sponsored by the Southern Christian Leadership Conference of the late Dr. Martin Luther King Jr.

Motorists drove with headlights blazing in the daylight as they have done since Kennedy's death. About one car out of four on the freeways had lights on.

Players on the Los Angeles Dodgers baseball team wore black armbands over their uniforms in tribute to the Senator.

Senator Henry M. Jackson, speaking at commencement exercises at Claremont Men's College, said, "Argument by gunfire is no way to conduct the business of democracy."

"In the aftermath of this tragedy, the whole nation must now take stock of the state of our society and of the attitudes and conditions that turn people to the lie that wrongs can be righted by taking the law into one's own hands," Jackson said.

U Thant: "Violence begets violence."

by Timothy Ferris

NEW YORK (UPI) . . . Secretary General U Thant and U.S. Ambassador Arthur Goldberg Sunday paid tribute to Senator Robert F. Kennedy and called for an end to the violence that caused his death.

In eulogies delivered at Holy Family Church, a block from the United Nations building, both men decried the "senseless" shooting which, in Thant's words, "deprives and diminishes us all."

Muhammad H. El-Farra, the Jordanian Ambassador to the U.N., sent a message to the 500 mourners gathered at the church. It said. "The Jordanian people are dismayed" by the Senator's death and offer condolences to the Kennedy family.

The Ambassador, scheduled to speak in person, was detained in Washington. His message was read by Muhammad Ali Khurma, the mission's charge d'affaires.

Thant told the gathering that all men share responsibility for Kennedy's death.

"We have seen too much violence everywhere to escape the responsibility which all must share for putting an end to it," the Secretary General said. "Violence begets violence, whether it takes the form of a massive war or an isolated assassination, an ill-considered appeal to violent emotions or the witless exploitation of violence as a form of public entertainment."

Goldberg said, "The terrible act of assassination all too vividly reminds us that the evils of violence and revenge still lie in men's hearts."

"We know these violent passions are wholly destructive of the good ends of peace and progress to which all nations and peoples aspire," Goldberg's message said.

Goldberg said, "Robert Kennedy had become a world figure, a renowned public servant, and the representative of a family great in leadership, and great also in bravely enduring misfortune."

"Robert Kennedy was young, not only in his years but in his outlook," Goldberg continued. "We who survive will not soon forget the shining example of his short life."

Later, as sunlight streamed through the modern stained-glass windows of the church, where a private mass for the Kennedy family was held Friday, Monsignor Timothy J. Flynn said that "a nation which tolerates violence in any form cannot expect to confine it to just minor outbursts."

Kennedy's chauffeur mugged

WASHINGTON (UPI) . . . A chauffeur for the late Senator Robert F. Kennedy said today he was beaten and robbed by seven youths early Sunday as he was returning home from the Senator's burial.

The driver, L. Edgar Morrow, 45, told police the youths took his wallet containing three gasoline credit cards in the name of the late Senator.

Morrow said the attack occurred when he parked near his Washington home after taking the Kennedy family to their McLean estate.

UN Secretary-General U Thant signs the "Respects Book" for Kennedy at the United Nations mission in New York while UN Ambassador Arthur Goldberg looks on.

Political Effects

Will the brutal deed in Los Angeles change the American way of politicking?

by Arnold B. Sawislak

WASHINGTON (UPI) . . . Few nations deserve to be judged solely by the quality of their politics. But of all the forms men have invented to govern, democracy is the quickest to boast of—and the least able to avoid responsibility for—the ideas, the men, and the methods it employs in the conduct of public affairs.

It is because of this that events such as the assassination of Senator Robert Francis Kennedy raise questions about the stability and direction, both in the short and long run, of the American political process.

The irony of American political violence is that it never has accomplished what the assassins seemed to want. Once, the death of a king might have ended a tyranny, but the course of a continental nation deeply immersed in world affairs and ruled by the elected representatives of its citizens does not change when one man dies.

Booth's cause was already lost and the South he professed to love suffered more when Lincoln died. Whatever the motives of John F. Kennedy's assassin, the great changes of mid-century American life were well under way and in some ways accelerated by the President's death.

And nothing could have been more futile than the murder of Robert Kennedy.

There was not the glimmering of a chance that Kennedy's death would change some important national policy. The nation's direction may be set by a President, but it can be continued only at the sufferance of the people. The change in the prosecution of the war in Vietnam was the most recent illustration of that.

True, the New York Senator had just surmounted an important obstacle in his effort to win the Presidency. But he was still second in the race after his California victory, and, by every sign available at the time, would have remained so when his party chose its Presidential candidate in August.

Ironically, the race would have entered a different, less public, phase after the June 4 California primary. California was the last of the big state contests in which the candidates had to conduct full scale election campaigns to seek convention delegate votes.

A new phase, in a manner of speaking, would have gone indoors—into the halls in states where party leaders and the rank-and-file choose or instruct their delegations by party convention.

About half of the Democratic and a smaller proportion of the Republican delegations remained to be selected. Campaigning for those votes is no less fierce, but certainly quieter, than in the primaries.

The first effect of the assassination was to make Vice President Hubert H. Humphrey an even stronger prospect for the Democratic nomination. It did not appear to make the slightest impact on the position of former Vice President Richard M. Nixon as the Republican leader.

Senator Eugene J. McCarthy gained some strength from those who followed Kennedy primarily for his opposition to the war. Governor Nelson A. Rockefeller of New York seemed more desirable to Republicans fearing a Democratic party united by tragedy. Governor Ronald Reagan of California probably won some new support for his strong theme of law and order.

At the time of the assassination, Humphrey was leading with 561½ delegate votes, Kennedy had 393½, McCarthy 255, and George C. Wallace 2, with 1,312 needed to nominate.

For the Republicans, with 667 required for nomination, Nixon had 392, Reagan 110, Rockefeller 77, and Harold E. Stassen 1.

It seemed apparent that Humphrey would get more of Kennedy's Democratic convention votes than McCarthy and that Nixon probably had the GOP nomination locked up.

One change in political life seemed likely. It was hard to believe that candidates, privately concerned but unwilling to act before the shooting over the risks of plunging into even the friendliest of crowds, would not pull back somewhat. President Johnson, who gave security men plenty to worry about in past campaigns, assured some new measure of orderly procedure and personal safety for the candidates by ordering Secret Service protection for all.

And many Americans, such as Republican National Chairman Ray Bliss, suggested that more television coverage be used to supplement the relentless face-to-face campaigning of the candidates.

In addition, there was hope for some deflation in political rhetoric and appeals calculated to excite partisan crowds. In this year, when a charge of inflaming prejudices might be more serious than ever before, the candidates were under strong pressure to choose their words with more care.

In the longer view, what of the "new politics" that both Kennedy and McCarthy said they were offering to the country?

Their idea, that citizens concerned enough to involve themselves in the political process could move the nation, was not new. "Participation politics" is what responsible Americans are supposed to be practicing all the time.

But this does not mean that Kennedy, and now McCarthy alone, did not have a grip on one of those large movements of history that change the course of events. If, for example, the "new politics" becomes the channel for the needs and demands of the poor, the minorities, and the young, it may indeed be a force that cannot be stopped by the loss of a leader.

Of course this would mean more conflict in American politics. Again, this would be no new phenomenon. From the first days of the Republic, the heat and, frequently, the light for the political process has been generated by the conflicting views of farmers and manufacturers, slaveholders and abolitionists, workers and employers, the poor and the wealthy.

And it cannot be denied that this competition has created passion, hate, and violence, especially during times of great social change. The record of four assassinated Presidents in itself is enough to show the long thread of violence in the U.S. political fabric.

Does this mean that murder must be reckoned as a potential price of public service in the United States? Unless the recent events have somehow shaken the hate out of American politics, it seems so.

If this is true, how can it be changed? Two ways come to mind. The first is to protect U.S. political leaders with platoons of openly armed men and keep them away from crowds. This seems unacceptable, if not to the leaders, then to the public.

The other way is to change the character of American politics, to soften the image of one candidate or party as the ultimate good and the other as evil incarnate. This would require Americans to believe that the application of force is not the way to resolve the conflict of ideas.

The future will follow the past. Like most of the other imperfect facets of their way of life, Americans have made their own politics.

ROBERT F. KENNEDY

1925-1968

*Some called him "ruthless"—yet he captured
the hearts of the young and downtrodden*

Controversy surrounded Robert Francis Kennedy throughout his public life, even up to the moment of his death. Yet, despite the criticism that came his way, it was his death that prompted an entire nation, friend and foe alike, to assess him in another light—that of a dedicated, hard-working man who, by the age of 42, had served two Presidents as Attorney General, was a Senator from New York, and a leading contender for the Democratic party's nomination for the Presidency itself.

As with his brother, John Fitzgerald Kennedy, whom he resembled so closely in appearance and speech, Robert Kennedy was destined by upbringing to take a role in the nation's life.

"Bobby," as his family called him, was born on Nov. 20, 1925, in the fashionable suburb of Brookline, Mass., to Joseph P. and Rose Kennedy. His father, the son of poor South Boston parents, was already amassing a personal fortune in the stock market and other enterprises.

Bobby was the "little brother." Joseph Jr. was 10 and John, later to be President, was 8 when he was born. (Edward was not born until 1932). There were sisters, too, all tomboyish. "I was," Robert Kennedy often conceded when called too aggressive, "the seventh of nine children. And when you come from that far down, you have to struggle to survive."

It was a struggle in both a physical and an emotional sense. His mother described him as "the smallest and thinnest." "We feared," she said, "he might grow up puny and girlish. We soon realized there was no fear of that."

It was his father, a controversial figure in his own day when he was Ambassador to the Court of St. James's, who fostered his competitive spirit, teaching him to sail, swim, and play baseball and football.

It was also his father who prodded his sons into political careers. John took over the mantle when Joseph Jr. died, and Robert fell heir to the family's aspirations when John died.

Overshadowed as a youth by his older brothers, Robert nevertheless displayed a grim determination to succeed. He attended Milton Academy, was never considered a brilliant student, but tried all the harder to succeed as a result. "It was much tougher for him than the others—socially, in football, with studies," a classmate remembered.

From Milton, Robert went on to Harvard University. He was a sophomore in 1944 when the first tragedy struck the Kennedy family: Joseph Jr. was killed in a Navy plane over the English Channel. On his own, Robert went to Washington and persuaded Navy Secretary James Forrestal to assign him as a seaman on a destroyer named after his brother.

Robert served out the war in the Caribbean. He returned to Harvard in 1946 and, despite being only 160 pounds and 5 foot 9, tenaciously gained a position as an end on the school's football team. He was graduated in 1948 and went on to law school at the University of Virginia, receiving his degree in 1951 as 56th in a class of 126. He was already interested in the world outside, so much so that the dean of the law school, Frederick D. G. Ribble, remarked, "I have the feeling that if he had been as much interested in high grades as in public affairs he would have been a very high-ranking student."

Robert went immediately into a government career upon graduation, joining the Criminal Division of the Justice Department in Washington and spending the next year and a half prosecuting graft and income-tax evasion cases without any special distinction, though his co-workers called him "bright." He resigned in 1952 to manage his brother John's campaign for the Senate in Massachusetts. It was a successful campaign, notable for the attention to detail and the amount of funds spent, two hallmarks of Robert's later campaign operations.

His first brush with controversy followed. In 1953, Robert was named one of 15 assistant counsels to the Senate Permanent Subcommittee on Investigations. His immediate superior was Roy M. Cohn. The committee was headed by Senator Joseph R. McCarthy, a Republican from Wisconsin. Robert had obtained the job through his father, who had donated funds to McCarthy's anti-Communist campaign. The Senator and the young lawyer got along well—to Robert's later embarrassment. But he and Cohn disagreed. Robert resigned in mid-1953 and, when he rejoined the committee in February of 1954, it was as counsel to the Demo-

At age 12, Bobby and younger brother Teddy, 6, entered Gibbs school in London where family lived while father Joseph P. Kennedy served as Ambassador to Great Britain.

Family Portrait 1937: Joseph P. Kennedy Sr. and his wife Rose are seated at left and right. The boys are, left to right, John, Robert, Edward, and Joe Jr. The girls are, left to right, Patricia, Jean, Eunice, Kathleen, and Rosemary.

Robert was sworn in as a Naval aviation cadet in 1943.

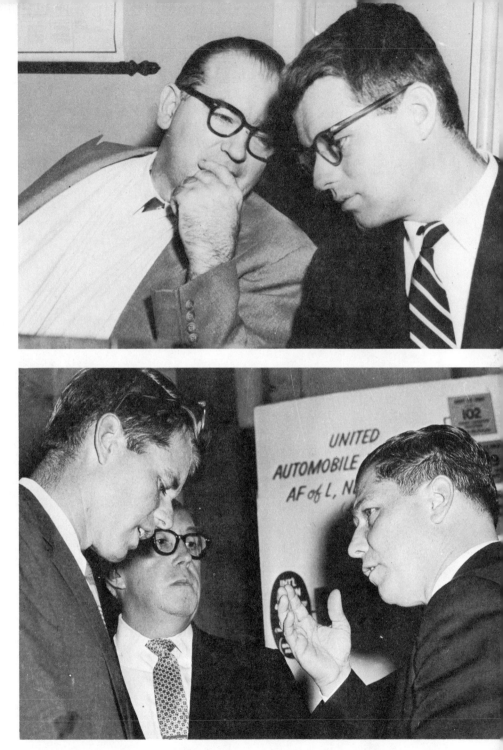

As a young lawyer in the 1950's, he became center of controversy, first as counsel for Senator Joseph R. McCarthy's Senate Investigation Subcommittee probing communism, top, and later as chief counsel for Senate Labor Rackets Committee. His determination in pursuing James Hoffa, president of the teamster's union, bottom, helped win him the label of "ruthless."

Family Portrait 1960: Seated, left to right, are his sister, Mrs. R. Sargent Shriver; parents; sister-in-law, Jacqueline; and brother, Edward. Standing, left to right, are his wife, Ethel; brother-in-law, Stephen Smith; sister, Mrs. Smith; brother,

John; Robert; sister, Mrs. Peter Lawford; brother-in-law, R. Sargent Shriver; sister-in-law, Mrs. Edward Kennedy; and brother-in-law, Peter Lawford.

As campaign manager for his brother, Kennedy conferred on the floor of the
1960 Democratic National Convention with his brother-in-law, Peter Lawford, left.

Kennedy served as Attorney General of the United States under both his brother and President Lyndon Johnson.

During John F. Kennedy's presidential administration, Robert was his brother's closest and most trusted adviser.